# Heritage

Nicola McCartney was artistic director of the Glasgow-based new-writing theatre company lookOUT from 1992 to 2002 and her plays for the company include *Laundry, Easy, Entertaining Angels, The Hanging Tree, Transatlantic* and *Home*. Other plays includes *The Millies* (Replay), *Cave Dwellers* (7:84 Scotland Theatre Co.), *Heritage* (Traverse), *For What We Are About to Receive* (Brunton Theatre), *Convictions* (Tinderbox) which won the Irish Times Theatre Awards Best Production, 2001, *Underworld* (Frantic Assembly), *Lifeboat* (Catherine Wheels) which won the TMA/Equity Best New Show for Children and Young People, 2002, *Standing Wave: Delia Derbyshire in the 60s* (Tron Theatre/Reeling & Writhing), *The Hero Show* (EGYTs), *A Sheep Called Skye* (National Theatre of Scotland) and *Bog People* (Big Telly Theatre Co). She was an inaugural associate playwright for the Playwrights' Studio Scotland in 2005, Creative Writing Fellow at the University of Edinburgh until 2008 and has had a number of writer-in-residence posts including University of Ulster and Shetland Arts.

As well as serving as a theatre director for many productions, including the award-winning 1996 tour of Harry Gibson's stage adaptation of *Trainspotting*, she has worked as dramaturg for a range of companies, including Vanishing Point, TAG, Theatre Hebrides, Theatre Cryptic, Stellar Quines and the Edinburgh International Festival, and has written widely for TV and radio. She received an SAC Creative Scotland Award in 2003.

# NICOLA McCARTNEY

# Heritage

*faber and faber*

First published in 2001
by Faber and Faber Limited
74–77 Great Russell Street
London WC1B 3DA

Typeset by Country Setting, Kingsdown, Kent CT14 8ES
Printed in England by CPI Bookmarque, Croydon, Surrey

A CIP record for this book
is available from the British Library

ISBN 978-0-571-21027-5

2 4 6 8 10 9 7 5 3

For my friends

*Thank you*

**Heritage** was first performed at the Traverse Theatre, Edinburgh, on 16 October 1998. The cast, in order of appearance, was as follows:

**Sarah** Iona Carbarns
**Michael** Joel Strachan
**Hugh McCrea** Iain Macrae
**Ruth McCrea** Rosemary Pelan
**Peter Donaghue** Eric Barlow
**Emer Donaghue** Mary McCusker

*Director* Phlip Howard
*Designer* Fiona Watt
*Lighting Designer* Renny Robertson
*Music* Gavin Marwick

# Characters

**Sarah**
a young emigrant from County Antrim, Ireland

**Michael**
Sarah's lover

**Hugh McCrea**
Sarah's father. About forty years

**Ruth McCrea**
Sarah's mother

**Peter Donaghue**
Michael's father. A farmer. A Canadian

**Emer Donaghue**
Irish. About eighty years

*Setting*
Farmlands surrounding the fictional township
of Stanley, Saskatchewan, Canada. The action
spans six years, from 1914 to 1920

# Act One

## ONE

*Fire. A boy dances, slowly at first, to the beat of a drum.*
*The dance grows more frenzied as the beat quickens.*
*Fire consumes the boy dancer.*
  *Silence.*

## TWO

*Early morning. The open fields of Saskatchewan.*
  *Sarah enters. Her clothes are spattered with an ashen*
*dust and her face and hands are dirty with the same.*
*Music.*

**Sarah**
  Nearly day.
  Sun bleeds morning over pigs and sheep and hens and
    goats
  Over the Land of the Shining Waters
  Over Canada
  Where we have come
  To reap the Wheat Boom.

  I will tell you the story.

  In the Wheat Country
  Winter comes hard
  And Spring comes harder
  Walking along river valley to home
  Pulling top coat chill-proof tight
  It is bitter
  No shelter
  Trees felled mercilessly

But still more trees than I remember from home
Ice twists on strange boughs of
Kentucky coffee
Tulip tree
Sassafras
Sycamore
Spruce
Jack pine
Red pine
White pine
Black walnut
Blue ash
Balsam fir
Basswood
Chinquapin oak
Sugar maple
Left in the rush of clearance
Sharp bite of the axe
Signal of settlement.
Boots heavy sludge through
Heavy clay soil
Each step a job of work
Panting
To the top of the rise
Breathless.

Below me
Vastness of the plain
Dotted with matchbox houses
Fields sleepin under white snow meltin
Spattered little brown patches where the plough went
   in late
Criss-cross sewn together with snake-rail fences
Muddy grey below stretches wide under muddy grey
   above
Forever.

*Springtime* 1914. *The pasture by the water.*
*Michael appears, carving a piece of wood.*

**Sarah**
I will tell you the story.
By the big river I met him
My boy
Mine
All mine
Top of the tallest tree and jump off boy
Fight boys twice his age and still win boy
Boy acted like he could take on the world with one
    arm tied behind his back.
Fearless, they called him.
Not cruel.
Never.
No sir, not he.
I will tell you the story.
Listen I will tell the story to you
As I have been told it.
I met him by the big river
In early Springtime
When the freeze of winter was on the turn
And they said that war was coming.
One day when she was out roaming the hills and fields
    round about,
Deirdre spied the young warrior,

**Sarah** *and* **Michael** 'Take me away from this place,'

**Michael** Said Deirdre. 'For you know that Conor the
King has sworn to take me as his bride. I have no desire
to spend the rest of my days wedded to an old man.'
'It is my *geis*, my solemn word of honour to rescue you,'
said Naoise. 'With the help of my brothers, the sons of
Usnach, I have got a boat. But we must go quickly. We
will leave this place tonight, my love, and never return.'
So, in the middle of the night they fled and set sail off the

northern coast. And Naoise wept as he left, for it was the land of his father. Across the sea he sailed to Scotland. There the Scottish king welcomed the warrior . . . /

**Sarah** / . . . Hey boy! What're you doin?

**Michael** Nothing.

**Sarah** I heard you talkin to yourself.

**Michael** Not me.

**Sarah** Only idiots and mad people talk to themselves . . . What were you sayin?

**Michael** Nothing.

**Sarah** What's that in your hand?

**Michael** Nothing.

**Sarah** You are one big nothing! Let me see.

**Michael** It's a boat.

**Sarah** 'S more the shape of a coffin than a boat. I bet it sinks like a stone . . . This is our land. You have no right to be playin in it.

**Michael** This land belongs to the Carews who've gone up to Vancouver. It's not sold yet.

**Sarah** It's as good as. My father has gone to the land agent today to bid for it.

**Michael** So has mine.

**Sarah** My father has one hundred acres this side of the water.

**Michael** My father has two hundred this side.

**Sarah** Get out of our river!

**Michael** No one owns the water. Except God. This is no river anyways. It's a stream.

**Sarah** It's a river. See, it reaches all the way into the distance.

**Michael** It doesn't matter how long it is but how wide. This cannot be a river because I can jump its width.

**Sarah** Go on then. Jump.

**Michael** No.

**Sarah** Do it – or I say that you're a liar.

**Michael** I am no liar.

**Sarah** Well, I say you are one and I say that this here is a river.

**Michael** It is a stream.

**Sarah** If you can't jump it, then you're a liar and must tell me the story.

**Michael** What story?

**Sarah** The one you were tellin to yourself just now.

**Michael** And if I can jump?

**Sarah** Then you're not a liar.

**Michael** But what do I get?

**Sarah** Your good name back.

**Michael** My name is good anyway. I want something else.

**Sarah** What?

**Michael** A kiss.

**Sarah** Get away! You'll have no such thing!

5

**Michael** Run home to your mama little cry-baby!

**Sarah** I am no cry-baby.

**Michael** Well, I say you are one. And a scaredy too!

**Sarah** And sure what's there to be scared of? (*A beat.*) Only if you jump the river.

*Michael attempts the jump and falls into the water.*

**Sarah** Tryin to walk on water now?

**Michael** Will you give me a hand?

*Sarah helps him.*

**Michael** You're right. It must be a river. Now we're on the same side.

**Sarah** Let go of my hand . . .

**Michael** I'll wait for my kiss then?

**Sarah** A kiss is a thing you'll never have from me. A cuff on the lug, maybe.

**Michael** So, you fight, girl?

**Sarah** Better than you.

*Sarah takes a swing at him. They tussle and she falls in the dirt.*

**Michael** That's fancy footwork! I don't blame you for mistaking this here for a river. I thought so too when I was a child.

**Sarah** I am thirteen years old and five months.

**Michael** Near as old as the century. That must make you very wise indeed.

**Sarah** Wise enough not to fall in a river.

**Michael** Just to fall on your ass in the dirt instead? . . . I am Michael Donaghue of Quebec, now of Stanley township, Saskatchewan.

**Sarah** Well, I can't say I'm pleased to meet you, Michael Donaghue.

**Michael** What do they call you?

**Sarah** Sarah McCrea, of Country Antrim, Ireland, now of Saskatchewan.

**Michael** You're John McCrea's younger sister.

**Sarah** How d'you know my brother?

**Michael** I fought him once.

**Sarah** What for?

**Michael** He called me a Papist bastard.

**Sarah** Are you?

**Michael** I'm a Papist – but no bastard.

**Sarah** Who won?

**Michael** He did. He broke my nose.

**Sarah** Good.

**Michael** But I cut his lip. So, Sarah McCrea of County Antrim now of Saskatchewan, what drove you here?

**Sarah** What?

**Michael** How come you to Saskatchewan?

**Sarah** All's I know is my father said he'd seen an advertisement offerin settlin on farms and the next thing I know, we're on a steamship out of Belfast.

**Michael** My grandmother came out of Derry on a sailing ship.

**Sarah** We sailed on the Cunard Line – passenger class. It took us near two weeks.

**Michael** My grandmother says the ocean is very big, bigger even than Lake Ontario.

**Sarah** Much, much bigger!

**Michael** Maybe the ocean gets smaller as you get bigger – just like the river?

**Sarah** I think the ocean will always be very big for my mother says you can only cross it the once and then it's for a lifetime.

**Michael** Is Ireland very green?

**Sarah** In summer it is. Why do you not go to the school?

**Michael** I'm too old.

**Sarah** The Martins are Catholics and they go.

**Michael** I didn't want to go and my father said I didn't have to if I didn't want.

**Sarah** I wish my father'd say that.

**Michael** What is Derry like?

**Sarah** I don't know. It's only on the other side of the country, as far as we are from Regina, maybe. Isn't that funny? Here I am in Canada, but I've never been to Londonderry. I've been to Belfast, though.

**Michael** I know nothing of Belfast except through the newspapers.

**Sarah** I was only there the once, on the way to the ship. We came in from the north of the city, down from the mountains, and there it was all spread out in front of us – the Lough, the linen mills and the factories. I thought it was the biggest, grandest place there was on earth until we passed through Toronto.

**Michael** I will go to Ireland one day.

**Sarah** Sure what'd you want to go there for?

**Michael** To see where I come from.

**Sarah** Canada is a far better country than Ireland.

**Michael** Do you think?

**Sarah** Yes, I do.

**Michael** Why's that?

**Sarah** Because . . . Because lots of reasons. Because you can grow peaches here. Tell me the story now.

**Michael** Why do you want to hear it?

**Sarah** I like stories.

**Michael** I will tell you the story as I have been told it. One night, Conor mac Nessa, King of Ulster, and his knights . . . /

**Sarah** / . . . Ulster's not a kingdom.

**Michael** It used to be.

**Sarah** When?

**Michael** A long time ago. Shall I tell you or not?

**Sarah** Go on and tell it.

**Michael** Without interruption? . . . Okay . . . One night Conor mac Nessa, King of Ulster, and his knights were feasting at the house of his chief poet, Felimidh. They ate and drank their fill and the great hall was full of the sounds of merrymaking. Felimidh's wife dutifully prepared the feast and played the hostess the whole night long, even though she was heavily pregnant. At last, filled with good food and ale, the guests began to fall asleep. Quietly, Felimidh's wife made her way through

9

the sleeping company to her own chamber, for the day had been a great strain for her . . .

*Ruth appears. Music.*

**Ruth** I will incline mine ear to a parable: I will open my dark saying upon the harp.

**Michael** . . . And great pain warned her that her child would soon be born.

**Ruth** Wherefore should I fear in the days of evil, when the iniquity at my heels shall compass me about?

**Michael** But passing through the great hall, the child in her womb gave out a cry . . .

**Ruth** They that trust in their wealth . . .

**Michael** A shriek so loud, that it roused the sleeping warriors . . .

**Ruth** And boast themselves in the multitude of their riches . . .

**Michael** Who seized their arms and rushed to see what it was that had made such a terrible sound.


### THREE

*Michael disappears.*
*Night of the same day. The McCrea farmstead. Sarah listens to Ruth reading from the family bible.*

**Ruth** . . . None of them can by any means redeem his brother, nor give to God a ransom for him: for the redemption of their soul is precious, and it ceaseth forever – that he should continue to live eternally and not see the pit. For he sees that wise men die . . . What's that?

*Sarah looks to see.*

**Sarah** It's not them.

**Ruth** Yorkton's not so far away that it should take them this long.

**Sarah** I wonder if they stopped off at the Millings'?

**Ruth** Why would they do that?

**Sarah** Maybe I should go and see.

**Ruth** Maybe you should be in your bed . . . For he sees that wise men die; likewise the fool and senseless person perish, and leave their wealth to others. Their inner thought is that their houses will continue forever, and their dwelling places to all generations . . . I worry for them, out and about this country so late and the roads in such a state.

**Sarah** Maybe they were ambushed?

**Ruth** What?

**Sarah** By Indians.

**Ruth** Oh, for pity's sake!

**Sarah** Mary Trimble was attacked by Indians.

**Ruth** No she wasn't. The Indians are all on reservations now.

**Sarah** Well, six of them come . . . /

**Ruth** / . . . Came. Six of them came.

**Sarah** Yes, while her father was away over to Yorkton to get the doctor for her mother who was sick in bed and near dyin.

**Ruth** I don't want to hear about it.

**Sarah** Mary and her two sisters had to hide under the bed while her brother stood guard with her father's hunting rifle. They thought they would all have their throats cut.

**Ruth** Sarah . . .

**Sarah** One of them was all painted and he came right up to the window and pressed his face against it with his eyes staring all wide and bloodthirsty – just like that!

**Ruth** Get away out of it! I let you sit up with me for company and this is what you do.

*Sarah picks up the bible.*

**Sarah** I was only sayin . . . Shall I read on?

**Ruth** Put it away.

**Sarah** How old is this?

**Ruth** You know how old it is.

**Sarah** Your mother's mother's.

**Ruth** It's raining now. The roads'll all be washed away.

*Sarah reads the inscription in the front of the bible.*

**Sarah** 'Ruth Milling *m.* Hugh Henry McCrea, November 1898 . . . 'This isn't your writing.

**Ruth** It's my mother's.

**Sarah** John Hugh, Sarah Elizabeth . . .

**Ruth** She wrote in all your names too. She had a beautiful hand.

*Hugh enters, carrying packages.*

**Hugh** By Jings, I'm knackered this night!

**Ruth** Hugh! Where've you been 'til this hour?

**Hugh** The roads is all churned up with the thaw. 'Twas heavy goin for the oul mare.

**Ruth** I told you not to be going away up there in this weather.

**Hugh** Were you worryin about me, my darlin? (*He embraces Ruth*.)

**Ruth** Get away out of this you old goat! . . . And take your boots off.

**Hugh** Yes, ma'am! (*to Sarah*) And how's my other girl?

**Sarah** I was watchin out for you.

**Hugh** I'm glad you was for I have plenty news to tell ye. Oh yes, indeed I have.

**Sarah** Tell me!

**Hugh** The wee boys all in bed?

**Ruth** Long ago. Which is where this one's going now.

**Sarah** Ach, Mammy!

**Hugh** Sure, let her sit up a while and have a yarn.

**Ruth** Never let it be said I was the one that spoiled her. Where's John?

**Hugh** He's takin the order back over to Samuel's.

**Ruth** At this hour? Could he not have waited til the morning?

**Hugh** I think he's got sweet on young Miss Rebecca Milling.

**Ruth** He's only a boy.

**Hugh** Fifteen years makes him near a man. He'd some sort of present he wished to deliver to the young lady. He wouldnae tell me what.

**Ruth** Wasting money he's no call wasting.

**Hugh** He even washed before he went out this mornin and I could hae sworn all these years he was feart o' water!

**Sarah** John's got a sweetheart!

**Ruth** Don't you be teasin him now.

**Hugh** And sure why would she be teasin him when she's got an admirer herself – young Master Robert Milling.

**Sarah** I can't marry him. He's my cousin.

**Ruth** He's fine looking.

**Sarah** He's too old.

**Ruth** He's not nineteen yet.

**Sarah** And he smells like a chimney with all that tobacco he smokes.

**Ruth** I never knew he smoked tobacco.

**Sarah** Sometimes he chews it up and spits it out.

**Hugh** Jays! That's desperate.

**Ruth** Hugh!

**Hugh** A vile habit.

**Sarah** I don't want him.

**Hugh** Good on ye.

**Ruth** She might be glad of somebody to take her, for she'll make no housewife.

**Sarah** Are you hungry, Daddy?

**Hugh** Starvin! My stomach feels like my throat's been cut.

*Sarah gets the food ready.*

**Ruth** Well, if you would come in for your meal at the proper time and not leave it spoiling . . .

**Hugh** And if I come in at the proper time you'd be complainin aboot all the work I hadnae done.

**Ruth** Wash your hands! (*to Sarah*) Be careful with that plate. Don't drop it!

**Sarah** I won't. (*Sarah sets the plate before Hugh.*)

**Hugh** Would ye look at that! Ham!

**Ruth** You've seen ham before.

**Hugh** I'm only sayin we're a damn sight better off . . .

**Ruth** Hugh! Mind your talk. (*to Sarah*) Don't let me hear you repeatin that.

**Hugh** . . . Better off where we are than where we were. (*He hands a package to Sarah.*) Here. This is for you.

**Ruth** Not more of those books.

**Hugh** Books is a good present.

  *Sarah unwraps the gift.*

**Sarah** *Western Girl's Companion!*

**Ruth** Filling her head with a load of old nonsense.

**Hugh** It's just stories.

**Ruth** She's bad enough as it is. She had you and our John attacked by Indians tonight.

**Hugh** No Indians is goin to attack your da – don't you worry!

**Sarah** Thank you, Daddy.

**Hugh** You can read to us ootay that later.

**Sarah** How was Yorkton?

**Hugh** Big and busy.

**Ruth** Did you get the cloth I asked for?

**Hugh** Aye.

**Ruth** And the lamp oil. (*He embraces Ruth again.*)

**Hugh** Give yourself peace, missus. I got all on your list.

**Ruth** What is all this cuddlin and getting on? Have you been at the drink?

**Hugh** I might ae had a wee nip tae celebrate.

**Ruth** Celebrate what?

**Hugh** Wait and hear. Sarah, where's my pen and writin paper?

**Sarah** Are we to write to Uncle William, Daddy?

**Hugh** We are. For we have news to tell and you shall write it, Sarah.

*Sarah finds the pen and paper.*

**Ruth** What's happened?

**Hugh** Wait and hear. (*to Sarah*) Set down the date first.

**Sarah** (*writing*) May 14th, 1914 . . .

**Hugh** Dearest brother William . . . (*A beat.*) There's a start. Let me look . . . Aye that's good. That's very good now. (*to Ruth*) The chile has a fair hand.

**Ruth** Aye, she can write, but she's slow with her other learning.

**Sarah** I do my best.

**Ruth** Aye, at sitting daydreaming! It's a wonder you've hands left on you at all with the number of slaps they've had for wandering attention.

**Hugh** Who's been baitin my chile?

**Sarah** That schoolteacher, Mister Rutherford, did the day.

**Hugh** For why?

**Sarah** I lost my place at the readin.

**Hugh** I thought you liked the readin?

**Sarah** I do.

**Ruth** Dreaming!

**Sarah** I wasn't dreaming. I was thinkin.

**Hugh** Isn't that desperate? Thinkin's what school's for, is it no? Well, you tell oul Rutherford that the next time he takes after ye with that strap your oul da will be down to that schoolhouse to knock him ontae his Scotch . . .

**Ruth** Hugh!

**Hugh** I was gonnae say 'back'.

**Ruth** You'll do no such thing. (*to Sarah*) And better still, the next time I hear you've had correction I'll give you the same myself when you get home, do you hear me?

**Hugh** Give the chile peace, missus. She'll be ootay school in six months and not need much figurin or letterin to keep a hoose.

**Sarah** What will I write to Uncle William, Daddy?

**Hugh** Now, let's see . . . I suppose we should tell him about the hoose . . . The new hoose is builded last summer, a wooden frame hoose of two storeys. Ruth has it all fitted out lovely.

**Ruth** Tell him I still favour the old-fashioned stone cottage above timber. I fear of fire in these houses.

**Hugh** I tell you what, Missus, I'll build ye a double-fronted hoose, a stoan hoose like the Millings' one day. Would that please ye?

**Ruth** It would.

**Hugh** Then I'll do it. And it will be twice as big and as tall as the Milling hoose and oor farm will be three times as big as their farm and Hugh McCrea will be four times as rich!

**Ruth** It's you she gets the dreaming from, indeed.

**Hugh** Is it now? (*to Sarah*) Set this down . . . Brother, I come back from the agent in Yorkton today havin bought myself another thirty acres of good land.

**Sarah** You got it!

**Hugh** I did so!

**Ruth** You did what?

**Hugh** I've bought part of the old Carew place. That makes one hunder'd and ninety acres of good fertile soil . . . What's that face for? You're not angered?

**Ruth** You would talk it over with a child before your wife?

**Hugh** I wanted to surprise you with it, Ruth.

**Ruth** How much did you pay for it?

**Hugh** Only eighteen dollars an acre.

**Ruth** Five hundred and forty dollars?!

**Hugh** It's good pasture land. The best for grazin cattle and the stream thereby.

**Ruth** We've only two milk cows, for pity's sake!

**Hugh** Aye, at the moment. But I reckon to buy another head and a bull with this year's harvest money.

**Ruth** If you can get a price for the wheat. How are you to afford it?

**Hugh** I went to see Hector Smyth at the bank.

**Ruth** Lord!

**Hugh** He's one of the brethren. He'll give me a good rate.

**Ruth** We're mortgaged up to our necks and still you're takin on more debt?

**Hugh** That's my affair. Never worry, missus.

**Ruth** How can you tell me not to worry, Hugh McCrea, when you go and do such things without asking me first?

**Hugh** And since when did a man have to seek permission from his wife to wipe his nose, eh?

**Ruth** He does when he's about to take the family into wreck and ruin.

**Sarah** Ma!

**Ruth** Keep your nose out!

**Hugh** Wreck and ruin?

**Sarah** Mammy . . .

**Ruth** Go to bed!

**Hugh** Stay where you are! (*to Ruth*) Wreck and ruin? . . . Jays, Missus, can you never be happy but you allus have to see the dark side of a thing? Look at these hands . . . Look! . . . These are the hands that signed the deed to this land. These are the hands that did the plantin and the buildin. These are the hands that the money passes intil and ootay again.

*Silence.*

**Ruth** Go to bed, Sarah.

**Hugh** I would have her sit up and finish the letter.

*A beat.*
*Sarah stays put. Hugh continues his dictation.*
*Music.*

**Hugh** God, Willy, I never knew I was alive until I got ootay Ireland and woke up! What a country this British North America is! Good land with the finest soil and all your own to do with as you see fit, with no older brother Henry at your back givin orders and no landlord to come and take his share of your toil at the month's end. There's been a small depression here of late but it has not hit us too hard as we huvnae got enough yet to lose. It was a right thing I done in comin here. If I had stayed home as you are doin, I would still be in rags workin the dirt and the mud with nothin to show for it. If only you would pluck up the courage and come too. I wonder would you send me some seeds of Balm of Gilead and also some of the lily? I have it in mind to sow a flower garden oot in frontay the hoose, a memory walk, so that Ruth can have all the colours and scents of home aboot her. You will wrap them in a piece of oiled paper, then fold your letter up, then paste them into the crease to hide them well. We will walk on the Twelfth this year again. Young John will play the flute – he is comin on well at it. The Orange Order is strong out here. Remember me to all the brethren. Write soon and send us news of home.

**Sarah** Will you mention Peggy, Daddy?

**Hugh** Surely we must mention her . . . As I'm sure you heard from Lizzie Milling, our youngest child, Margaret, died from the pneumonia, aged two years, this Christmas last. The winters is very severe here. Remember me also to brother Henry and family.

**Ruth** Don't sign my name to it, if you're writing to that one. (*Ruth exits.*)

**Hugh** Would you rather be back in Ireland, Sarah?

**Sarah** I like it here.

**Hugh** Good girl! Let's see now. (*He examines the letter.*) That's fine! Isn't that fine, Ruth? . . . (*to Sarah*) You're a clever one, aren't ye? I must sign my name to it now.

*Hugh writes.*

**Hugh** Yours . . . with . . . affectation . . .

**Sarah** Affection, Daddy.

**Hugh** Aye . . . Your brother, Hugh . . . . That's good. (*to Sarah*) Now write on the envelope – to Master William McCrea, McCrea's Farm, Ballinderry Road, near Ballymoney, County Antrim, Ireland.


FOUR

*Late September 1914. Sarah walking through the pasture, by the water. Michael jumps out at her.*

**Michael** Heah!

*He throws her a stick.*

**Sarah** Who goes there?

**Michael** I am Naoise, Red Hand Knight of Ulster.

**Sarah** You cannot step upon this shore.

**Michael** Me and my bride seek refuge here with the Scottish king.

**Sarah** Stay and prove yourself!

*They 'sword fight'.*

**Sarah** You waited.

**Michael** I had nearly given you up. What kept you?

**Sarah** Oul Rutherford made me stay behind.

**Michael** On your last day? What for?

**Sarah** Knocking over a pile of books.

**Michael** Clumsy!

**Sarah** Got you!

**Michael** Mercy!

**Sarah** Die!

**Michael** It's not in the story that you kill me.

**Sarah** I will spare you and your bride. Stay here and live as my brother.

**Michael** In return for this I pledge my allegiance and skills as a warrior to your service. Say who has offended the honour of our Protector?

**Sarah** Mister Rutherford.

**Michael** Death to Mister Rutherford!

**Sarah** No more Mister Rutherford!

*They flay away at an imaginary Mister Rutherford with their sticks.*

**Michael** What did you learn?

**Sarah** Countries and their capitals. I got them all right and oul Rutherford says, 'It's a wonder, Miss McCrea, for though you have now reached the age of fourteen I had doubts you could count to that number.'

**Michael** I'll test you.

**Sarah** I'm done with school.

**Michael** Turkey?

**Sarah** That's a hard one.

**Michael** Istanbul . . . Great Britain?

**Sarah** Too easy.

**Michael** Canada?

**Sarah** I'm not stupid.

**Michael** France.

**Sarah** Paris.

**Michael** Italy?

**Sarah** Rome. Harder!

**Michael** Egypt?

**Sarah** I don't know that one.

**Michael** It's Cairo, stupid!

**Sarah** I am not stupid! Another!

**Michael** Bosnia?

**Sarah** Sarajevo, where the Duke got shot and the war started.

**Michael** Very good. The master was right – you're not as stupid as you look.

**Sarah** Mister Rutherford said that it is Canada's duty to give whatever help she can to the efforts of the Allies on the Western Front.

**Michael** Russia?

**Sarah** You can volunteer.

**Michael** I don't want to.

**Sarah** Why not? You're old enough. Our John will go as soon as he is sixteen.

**Michael** Of course he will. He'd enjoy killing people.

**Sarah** That's a terrible thing to say.

**Michael** Running Huns through the ribs with his bayonet.

**Sarah** He's a damn sight braver than you.

**Michael** I won't fight. For it is not our war.

**Sarah** It's a threat to the British Empire.

**Michael** This is Canada. (*He gives her a present – a handkerchief.*)

**Michael** Happy birthday!

**Sarah** You've no call givin me presents.

**Michael** D'you like it?

**Sarah** It's pretty. Did you sew it yourself?

**Michael** I found it. In my grandmother's linen chest.

**Sarah** Will she not miss it?

**Michael** It belonged to my mother, I think. See the little flowers?

**Sarah** Lilies. Thank you.

**Michael** It's okay.

*She kisses him.*

**Michael** I am Conor mac Nessa, King of Ulster. Where is Felimidh my chief bard?

**Sarah** Here I am, sire!

**Michael** You have pleased us, Felimidh, with this feast and these revels. We will now retire to our chamber for the night.

**Sarah** I will be Felimidh's wife. The feast is over and she is very tired.

**Michael** Passing through the great hall . . . /

**Sarah** / . . . What's her name?

**Michael** She doesn't have one.

**Sarah** She must have a name.

**Michael** She is called Felimidh's wife.

**Sarah** That's not a proper name.

**Michael** All right! Ethne . . . Passing through the great hall, the child in her womb . . .

**Sarah** Ethne's womb.

**Michael** . . . gave out a cry, a shriek so loud, that it roused the sleeping warriors. Felimidh feared the men at arms. (*He plays Felimidh now.*) 'It was the scream of my wife's unborn child that has wakened you,' he said (*a warrior*). 'Call your wife before us,' said the chief warrior. Trembling with fear . . .

**Sarah** This is my part.

**Michael** She was so frightened that she could only answer . . .

**Sarah** No mother knows what sleeps in her womb.

**Michael** That's right! But, later that night, she gave birth to a child – a girl child with shining eyes and fair hair. Cathbad the Druid prophesied over her. 'You, O Deirdre of the Sorrows . . .

**Sarah** You can't be all the parts.

**Michael** You are Felimidh's wife. That's the only girl in this bit of the story.

**Sarah** I want to be the Druid.

**Michael** You don't know how to be the Druid. You don't even know what a Druid is.

**Sarah** I do too . . . It's a sort of magician.

**Michael** No. A Druid is a seer.

**Sarah** Like a fortune-teller or a tinker?

**Michael** Sort of, but grander.

**Sarah** That's easy.

**Michael** Okay, you be Cathbad . . . The Druid took the baby – gently – in his arms and prophesied over her.

*A beat.*

**Sarah** What do I say?

**Michael** How can you be Cathbad if you don't know the words?

**Sarah** Because you will tell me. Come on!

**Michael** You, O Deirdre of the Sorrows.

**Sarah** You, O Deirdre of the Sorrows.

**Michael** Will grow up into a beautiful young woman.

**Sarah** Will grow up into a beautiful young woman.

**Michael** Vivid as a flame.

**Sarah** Vivid as a flame.

*Peter enters, unseen by them, and listens.*

**Michael** So beautiful, that you will bring great sorrow to the province of Ulster.

**Sarah** So beautiful, that you will bring great sorrow to the province of Ulster . . . How was that? Did I make a good Druid?

**Michael** You were okay. A bit too fairground perhaps. The warriors, alarmed by such a dread prophecy, immediately demanded the child's death that Ulster would be spared this fate.

**Sarah** But then, Conor the King spoke forth.

**Peter** 'I decree that the child be sent far away from Emain Macha, to be reared by a nurse until marriageable age. Then I will take her as my queen,' he declared. And he sent her out of harm's way to a lonely place to be raised by a nurse, the poet, Levercham, who taught her many things, and a poor herdsman was her foster father.

**Sarah** It's a good story.

**Peter** It is.

**Sarah** I had never heard it before Mike told it to me.

**Peter** I'm sure you hadn't. (*to Michael*) Where've you been? You've been gone since dinner. You know there's baling to be done yet.

**Michael** I lost track of time.

**Peter** It's nearly supper. Who's your friend?

**Sarah** Sarah McCrea.

**Michael** Sarah, this is my father, Peter Donaghue.

**Sarah** Hello.

**Peter** Pleased to meet you, Miss McCrea. So you're the one my son neglects his work for. He's been keeping you a secret.

**Sarah** Are you ashamed of me?

**Michael** No.

**Sarah** I'm sorry to keep him from his work. He came to meet me after school, but I was late.

**Peter** It's not your fault that he's work-shy.

**Sarah** I just finished at the school today, you see.

**Michael** It's her birthday.

**Sarah** I wanted Mike to come celebrate with me.

**Peter** Well, I hope you take to whatever occupation you choose better than my son has took to farming.

**Michael** I'm sorry about the baling.

**Peter** No matter. Plenty more work tomorrow. Come on! I'd rather fight in the trenches any day than face your grandmother when late for supper.

**Michael** Can Sarah come to supper with us?

**Peter** I expect she has a home of her own to go to.


FIVE

*Music.*
   *Ruth plants seeds in the memory walk.*


SIX

*Later: the Donaghue farmstead.*

**Emer**
   It come on so sudden
   Morning
   Mist rises up out of the lough
   Hovers over.
   Day before, potatoes good
   Now leaves all black
   Crumble into ashes
   Palm-stain dark.

Air hanging heavy
Smell of sickness
Smell of death.
Fields all weepin-wailin women and children
My daddy, poor cottier
Lost foot on the land.
The British!
Not even a crust of bread to chew upon they give us
Ship off cattle and grain we've raised to serve up on
  English dinner tables
While our children
Perish.
Protestant ministers! They dishin out bowls of free soup
But you must recant
Must throw away soul.
So we live on –

**Emer** and **Michael**
Grass, seaweed and shellfish.

*Michael and Sarah listen to Emer. Peter working away
at his ledger.*

**Emer** That was the beginning of the great disease that
destroyed Ireland, Mihal.

**Sarah** What's recant?

**Michael** To turncoat on our Catholic faith.

**Emer** That's right, son.

**Michael** They say some ate human corpses.

**Sarah** They ate the dead people?

**Peter** God in heaven!

**Emer** I never saw that now. But they say some turned
cannibal. No one can know what we suffered. I pray to
God that you and yours may never know.

**Peter** Mike! You were walking the top fifty acres this morning?

**Michael** Yes.

**Sarah** (*to Emer*) And then you came to Canada?

**Emer** For five pounds passage each we sailed on the ship Superior out of Derry on the thirteenth of July, eighteen forty-nine.

**Peter** (*to Michael*) Notice any damage?

**Michael** Don't think so.

**Peter** You sure?

**Michael** Sure, I'm sure.

**Emer** We sailed into Quebec City on the fourth of November. I was eleven years old.

**Sarah** That's the age I was when we came here. We sailed on the Cunard Line.

**Emer** Coffin ships, they called them.

**Peter** Good.

**Emer** But all my family survived it.

**Peter** So, one hundred and ten acres at forty bushels an acre, that makes . . .

**Emer** Peadar! We are talking.

**Peter** Excuse me.

**Emer** My father really wanted to go to Philadelphia.

**Peter** Four-four-oh at ninety-three cents a bushel . . .

**Sarah** Why?

**Peter** The great Republic.

**Emer** But it was too expensive.

**Peter** Makes two thousand and twenty-eight dollars with tax and a bit more off. (*to Michael*) That's good isn't it?

**Michael** Yeah.

**Peter** Better than last year. How's your father's harvest, Sarah?

**Sarah** Not as big as that, I think.

**Emer** Ah, we should have gone to America at last.

**Peter** Liberty and justice for all.

**Emer** Thousands were driven out by the Great Hunger.

**Peter** They leaving in their droves long before that, mother. Opportunity forced them out long before a bit of potato blight.

**Emer** You remember all this, Mihal. It is where you come from.

**Peter** He was born in Canada. He was raised in Canada. He will work to pay his taxes to the Canadian government. He is Canadian.

**Michael** *Cuimhnigh ar sin, a mhicil.*[1]

**Sarah** *Cuimhneoidh mé a mhamó.*[2]

**Peter** Don't start on that.

**Michael** Tell about the uprising.

**Emer** The Young Irelanders?

**Michael** This is a good one.

**Peter** Oh yes! Tell us about the Young Irelanders. That was a great and glorious uprising, Sarah. Somebody's

---

[1] You remember all this, Michael.

[2] I will remember, Grandma.

gun went off by mistake and another paddy lost his shovel in a County Tipperary cabbage patch.

**Emer** Your father was in the Movement.

**Peter** The sins of my father are not mine to be judged for.

**Emer** Holy God! Your father was no sinner. There was never a finer man . . . /

**Peter** / . . . Here we go!

**Emer** Never a finer man than him. And I'll not sit here and listen to this, you, you – traitor!

**Peter** Then go to bed.

**Emer** No respect! He has none.

**Peter** I have respect for facts and truth.

**Emer** We should've stayed in Quebec beside our friends.

**Peter** On the good British land granted you by the good British government? You and my father were happy to take that, weren't you? Be careful of history, Sarah.

**Emer** Bringing us away out here to be surrounded by Puritans.

**Peter** History's more dangerous a friend than an enemy.

**Emer** You always were a lover of the British.

**Peter** Don't.

**Emer** She was no good. No good.

**Peter** Nothing but a load of lies and bitterness.

**Emer** *Ní féidir faic insint duitse.*[3]

---

3 You couldn't tell him anything.

**Michael** *Céard faoi a bhfuil tu ag caint?*[4]

**Emer** *Is cuma, a mhic.*[5]

**Peter** We have company.

**Michael** You're talking about my mother aren't you?

**Peter** She hardly knew your mother.

**Michael** *Ba mbaith liom fios a bheith agam.*[6]

**Emer** *Bhí sí posta cheanna.*[7]

**Peter** She was a widow.

**Michael** *An raibh?*[8]

**Emer** *Niorbh fhéidir caint leis; thug mé rabhadh dhó. Thug a athair rabhadh dhó.*[9]

**Peter** Michael, it's time for Sarah to be going home.

**Michael** It's not late yet.

**Peter** I think it is.

**Michael** *Céard atá i gceist agat? Abair liom, a mhamó!*[10]

**Emer** *Iarr ar d'athair.*[11]

---

4 What are you talking about?

5 No matter, son.

6 I want to know.

7 She was married before.

8 Was she?

9 There was no talking to him either; but I warned him. His father warned him.

10 What do you mean. Tell me, Grandma!

11 Ask your father.

**Michael**  *Ni insionn sé faic domsa.*[12]

**Peter**  In English, the pair of you! (*to Michael*) There's nothing I haven't told you.

**Emer**  Where is she now, eh?

**Peter**  Wherever she is, she's getting peace and rest.

**Emer**  Better than she deserves.

**Michael**  *Céard atá i gceist agat?*[13]

**Peter**  Will you stop!

**Sarah**  I'd best go, Mike.

**Peter**  I'm sorry, Sarah. Michael will take you home in the wagon.

**Michael**  I want to know what she means.

**Peter**  She's confused.

**Emer**  My mind's as sharp as a razor.

**Peter**  Your tongue is. (*to Michael*) Take your friend home. It's late.

**Sarah**  Thank you for supper.

**Emer**  No trouble.

**Sarah**  Can I come again?

**Emer**  *B'fhearr e mura dtiocfadh se' anseo aris coiche.*[14]

**Michael**  *Cén fath?*[15]

---

[12] He never tells me anything.

[13] What do you mean?

[14] It's better she doesn't come here again.

[15] Why?

**Emer** *Bí curamach a mchicil, maidir le céard atá a dhéabamh agat.*[16]

**Peter** Sarah is always welcome here.

**Sarah** Thank you. Goodnight.

**Michael** I want to know what she means.

**Peter** Another time. Good night. And don't be late home. You'll have to rise early to make up the work from today.

**Michael** Okay, okay! *Slán a mhamó.*[17]

*Michael and Sarah exit.*

**Emer** *Slán a mhic . . . . A Dhía dhilis!*[18] Goin the same way as you. Every bit of him.


SEVEN

*Summer 1915.*
*The Twelfth of July parade. Yorkton.*
*Music.*

**Sarah**
Dubadum dubadubadum
Dubadum dubadubadum
Big lambeg beats
Boom boom
Boom boom
One head made of ass's skin could shatter a window
And boom and boom and boom boom boom!

---

[16] Be careful of what you are doing, Michael.

[17] Goodbye, Grandma.

[18] Goodbye, son . . . God in Heaven!

Shudders and shakes you to the liver
High G on the D flute
Thrill of pain it gives you in the heart
Brother John marchin, puffin, whistlin
Isn't he doin well?
Go on, John!
It is old but it is beautiful and its colours they are fine . . .
Banners unfurl under trees green
Sons of William, Orange
Loyal Sons of Canada, gold
Fluttering by
Dubadum dubadubadum
Boom boom
Dubadum dubadubadum
Boom boom
For heh-ho!
The lily-o!
The royal orange lily-o!
King Billy on a white charger leading Sunday Best
    parade
Sashes, all fire-colour marching
Past women in hats
And girls in frocks
And wee boys in long trousers
Waving
And singin our songs
Man with lance
Man with bible
Our bible
Man with white gloves and a big sword
With ting and toot and crash and boom we'll guard
    old Derry's walls!
Marching
To the field.

Our field
Of cake and ginger beer

And aniseed drops
And candy sticks
And kick the can
And hide and seek
And sing on a rope
And red, white and blue
Our day out
Of tea and sandwiches
And cold meats and currant buns
And summer salad
And little nips of whiskey while the women's backs are
    turned.
And let us pray.
Our Father which art in heaven
And the Lord's my Shepherd
And God bless Sir Edward Carson
And God save our gracious King
And Ireland shall never submit to Home Rule
And Ulster will fight and Ulster will be right
And God bless our forces on the Western Front
And keep the Empire Protestant.
Oh God, our help in ages past
Our hope in years to come
Our day.

## EIGHT

*Night. McCrea farmstead. Twelfth of July, summer 1915.
Ruth and Sarah sewing. Hugh raises his glass of whiskey
in a toast.*

**Hugh** To the glorious and immortal memory of King
William of Orange who saved Ireland from Popes and
Popery and from brass money and wooden shoes. And
to any man who denies this toast, may he be rammed,
slammed and jammed into the Great Gun of Athlone

and fired into the Pope's belly and the Pope into the Devil's belly and the Devil into Hell and the door locked and the key thrown away forever!

**Ruth** Will you mind your talk? (*to Sarah*) Have you not that finished yet?

**Sarah** It's near done.

**Ruth** Can you manage?

**Sarah** It's only a few oul socks, Ma.

**Ruth** Let me see . . . What's this?

**Sarah** What's wrong with it?

**Ruth** (*to Hugh*) Will you look at that?

**Hugh** Don't ask me now. Nothin at all to do with me.

**Ruth** (*to Sarah*) How many times do I have to tell you? Small stitches, even stitches.

**Hugh** Sure, big or small makes no difference as long as it all holds together.

**Ruth** You want holes in your clothes, do you? (*to Sarah*) Give it to me.

**Sarah** I can fix it.

**Ruth** Just let it be.

**Sarah** I'll start over.

**Ruth** Leave it alone, I tell you! Leave it alone . . . It's a disgrace you are to me. A disgrace.

*A beat.*

**Hugh** Who d'ye think was askin after ye today at the Field, Sarah?

**Sarah** I don't know.

**Hugh** Robert Milling.

**Sarah** Sure, what was he askin you for? He saw me himself.

**Hugh** He was askin me if you was walkin out with anybody. I said, 'No.' That's right, isn't it?

**Sarah** It is.

**Ruth** Of course it is.

**Hugh** And then he asked me if he could coort ye.

**Sarah** And what did you say?

**Hugh** I told him ye were too young yet. 'Come back when she's forty,' says I. 'That'll be time enough for her to be thinkin of coortin.'

*He takes another drink.*

**Ruth** (*to Sarah*) Well, you needn't think you're sitting here 'til you're forty. No help to me at all. (*to Hugh*) No more now.

**Hugh** Missus, I'm on my holidays.

**Ruth** You've had enough to drown the fish.

**Hugh** Ah, sure, there's one or two of them no deid yet!

**Sarah** It was a big parade the day, Daddy.

**Hugh** It was.

**Ruth** Our John did well.

**Hugh** He did; though I think he hit a few notes wrong in the Lilly Balero. Jays, my ears was ringin!

**Ruth** He did not!

**Hugh** I'm tellin ye. Aye . . . It was a grand day.

**Sarah** How d'ye join the Orange, Daddy?

**Ruth** Don't be stupid! You know women cannot join.

**Sarah** Why not?

**Ruth** Because it's only for the men.

**Hugh** In case we have to fight.

**Sarah** For what?

**Hugh** For the Empire.

**Sarah** I don't see the need for it away out here.

**Ruth** Who's been filling your head with talk like that?

**Sarah** It's my own opinion.

**Hugh** She's havin opinions now!

**Ruth** That's what comes from too much talk.

**Hugh** Well, here's an opinion for you: this here is British North America. We're no republic here yet.

**Sarah** I'm sorry.

**Hugh** It hurts me to hear you speak like that . . . (*A beat.*) Come here and tell us one of your stories.

**Sarah** Which one shall I tell you?

**Hugh** Any one you like.

**Sarah** I've a new one. It's about Ulster. I hadn't heard it until I came here. Isn't that strange? . . . It happened many years ago. One stormy night, after a fierce battle, Conor the King was feasting at the house of his poet, Felimidh. A child was born to Felimidh's wife and . . . /

**Ruth** / . . . What story's this?

**Sarah** The story of Deirdre of the Sorrows. Do you know it?

**Ruth** I do not. Where did you hear that?

**Sarah** . . . At school once.

**Ruth** I don't think so.

**Sarah** It's about Ulster.

**Ruth** I don't want to hear it.

**Sarah** Why not, Ma?

**Ruth** Because it's not in our heritage, Sarah.

**Sarah** But we're Irish.

**Ruth** Our ancestors were Scottish. We are Irish – but we're British too.

**Sarah** And now we're living in Canada. So what does that make us?

**Hugh** We're Scots Irish Canadian British subjects, Sarah. That's what we are.


NINE

*Sarah alone.*
  *Music. Sound of war.*

**Sarah**
  Heritage
  A brand burned deep through skin of centuries
  Scarring forever
  The soul
  The land
  The memory
  The future
  Carried across deathbeds
  Across oceans to faraway lands
  Burning deep into the soil
  Blood in the veins

And fire in the blood
What fire!
Sixty thousand miles from here
Big guns go
Boom boom
Boom boom
At Ypres
Canadians
French
British
Irish
All
Defending the Empire
Boom boom
Sixty thousand miles away
They harvesting and reaping and planting the dead
Sixty thousand miles away
From planting and harvesting and profit.


TEN

*Late summer 1915. The McCrea farmstead.*
*Hugh is building a new barn.*

**Sarah**
Ten cows now
Twenty sheep
And one hundred and ninety acres
Planted
Corn, oats and wheat
Farm laid out in strict rectangle
Wooden-frame house at one end
Stable here
Outhouse on this side
Here – orchard
That will grow apples, plums, cherries and

Peaches.
There – vegetable garden
Leeks, beets, carrots, potatoes, cabbages, grapes,
    melons, squash
In front
Orange lilies in the memory walk
Sown from crease of the letter seeds from home.
And now
The barn.

**Hugh** Here we go! One, two, three – lift!

**Sarah** Progress.

*Hugh shouts to his men (offstage).*

**Hugh** I need two more men on the back walk. Two,
I said! You! And you! Come on, let's go.

**Sarah**
    Men from Italy
    Doukhobours and Ruthenians
    Irish men
    Orange men
    To build the new barn
    Log on log
    Plank on plank
    Up and up
    Tower of Babel.

**Hugh** You! Get me two ropes!

**Sarah**
    Ready for harvest
    Ready to hold the wheat of
    Boom boom
    Wheat boom.

**Hugh** No! Ropes, man! Ropes! Does anybody speak
English here?

**Sarah**
   Tap tap tap
   Whistle of saw through wood
   Rhythm of the future

**Hugh** All hands to the pump! Sarah! You know how to drive a nail home, don't ye?

**Sarah** Yes, Daddy.

**Hugh** Well, get to it. John! Reach me my claw hammer. Hurry up! I'm tellin ye, no one's raised a barn so quick as this.

**Sarah**
   My nail goes in
   Bang!
   South wall facing
   America.

   *Ruth enters.*

**Ruth** Sarah!

**Hugh** She's helpin me.

**Ruth** Indeed she's not. (*to Sarah*) I thought I asked you to lift beets for the dinner.

**Sarah** I'll do it now.

**Ruth** Hurry up! There's eight hungry men to feed.

**Hugh** D'ye know what I'll do when I've finished the barn? I'll dig out foundations for the stoan hoose. Would that please you?

**Ruth** If we could afford to pay for it.

**Hugh** We'll pay for it twice over with the way things is goin. Wheat prices is over one dollar a bushel. I reckon on near to thirty bushels an acre. That makes near . . .

**Ruth**  A thousand dollars.

**Hugh**  Aye. Wi' taxes and all considered. That'll pay the note on the land and a bit besides.

**Sarah**  There's somebody comin up the road!

**Hugh**  Who is it?

**Sarah**  Mister Donaghue . . . And Michael!

**Ruth**  What're they doing here?

**Hugh**  Now! We have to be neighbourly. Donaghue's a polite, quiet sort of a fella. The Catholics here is of a differ'nt nature to the Irish ones.

**Ruth**  They're just as sleekit here as anywhere.

*Peter and Michael enter.*

**Hugh**  Good day.

**Peter**  Good day to you. Are you well?

**Hugh**  Couldn't be better. Yerself?

**Peter**  Well enough. It's a scorcher.

**Hugh**  'Tis that. You remember my wife, Ruth?

**Peter**  Missus McCrea.

**Ruth**  Mister Donaghue. How is Missus Donaghue?

**Peter**  Oh, fighting fit.

**Ruth**  Give her my regards, won't you?

**Peter**  She'll be pleased to receive them. This is my son, Michael.

**Michael**  Hello, sir. Missus.

**Hugh**  We know him.

**Ruth**  Sarah, away and get those beets for me.

**Sarah** Yes, Ma.

**Ruth** Now!

*Sarah moves a safe distance off, keeping eye contact with Michael.*

**Peter** Hard to work in this.

**Ruth** The heat would kill you, so it would.

**Peter** Looks like it (*the barn*) is gonna be a skyscraper.

**Hugh** Biggest I know of in the township.

**Peter** You must be expecting a good harvest.

**Hugh** I've busted my back getting every acre I have broken and planted. I have hope.

**Peter** Yes. 'S a fine place you have here.

**Hugh** Three years of hard work.

**Peter** Have you enough men?

**Hugh** There's myself and young John, and Lightbody and Trimble there from the Lodge, and a couple of Russian fellas. The two Italians is bloody useless. (*shouting offstage*) No! Not that way! Turn it round! God's sake . . .

**Peter** If you need any more pairs of hands, Mike and myself are willing. Aren't we, Mike? . . . Mike!

**Michael** What?

**Peter** I said, we're willing to help.

**Michael** Yeah.

**Hugh** That's very daicent of ye.

**Peter** Ah well. We're all in the same boat out here, aren't we?

**Hugh** We are indeed.

**Ruth** I must away and get the dinner on.

**Hugh** Will ye stay with us and have a bite?

**Peter** If we're welcome.

**Ruth** Of course you're welcome . . . Sarah!

**Sarah** I'm doin it.

*Ruth exits.*

**Peter** Where shall we start?

**Hugh** Well, I could use another big man like yerself on the back wall and the boy here can help our John with the door frame.

**Peter** You're the boss man. Got enough tools?

**Hugh** Another hammer wouldn't go amiss.

**Peter** There's one in the wagon. (*to Michael*) Well, go on. Go and help John.

*Michael exits.*

**Hugh** I think they've had disagreements.

**Peter** That one disagrees with everybody – even himself.

*The two men begin work.*

**Sarah**
    Tap tap tap
    Noonday sun overhead
    High
    One wall raised
    Another begins
    I
    Fingers scrabble through dirt
    Pulling up from earth

*Michael enters.*

**Michael** Your brother's driving me crazy!

**Sarah** What's he doin?

**Michael** He keeps whispering at me.

**Sarah** What's he whisperin?

**Michael** Papist! Papist!

**Sarah** Is that all? He's only teasin you.

**Michael** He's a fool. Twice he's belched in my face.

**Sarah** I'll get him for you later if you like. I always get him back when he's sleepin.

**Michael** I can defend myself. If I could just take a swing at him, I'd crack that idiot grin of his.

**Sarah** Then do it and stop talkin about it.

**Michael** Come away!

**Sarah** I have to do this.

**Michael** Come on! Up to the river. We'll go swimming.

**Sarah** It's all dried up.

**Michael** Come for a walk then.

**Sarah** I have to do this.

**Michael** I can't work in this heat.

**Sarah** D'you want to land me in trouble?

**Michael** Don't talk to me then, if you don't want to.

**Sarah** I want to.

**Michael** Why is your barn so big?

**Sarah** Because my father wants it to be.

**Michael** It's four times the size of your house.

**Sarah** He's goin to build a bigger house. Out of stone.

**Michael** No one builds their houses out of stone here.

**Sarah** It's what *she* wants. And what she wants she gets.

*Michael exits.*
*The men working.*

**Sarah**
Tap tap tap
Build it up higher
Passing hand to hand.

*Hugh sips a mug of water.*

**Peter** It's a piece of work.

**Hugh** We'll have it filled to the brim in no time.

**Peter** That door frame's crooked.

**Hugh** What?

**Peter** That join there. The upright is cut at a steeper angle than the crosspiece. See? The edges don't sit smooth together.

**Hugh** I wouldn't have noticed that.

**Peter** Until you tried to hang the doors. Then the whole frame would twist and leave a gap for the wind to come and blow away your wheat.

**Hugh** Honest to God . . . Young ones allus does things in a hurry. (*shouting offstage*) John!

**Peter** No use asking them to do it. May as well do it ourselves and do it proper.

**Hugh** Aye.

**Peter** The heat is surely blazing.

**Hugh** Here. (*He hands Peter the mug of water.*) It's very good of you to help us out like this. You're a good woodworker.

**Peter** It was my trade before farming – one of them, anyway.

**Hugh** How many trades have you had?

**Peter** Carpenter, cooper, railroad digger. And prospector.

**Hugh** You were at Dawson City?

**Peter** Not for long.

**Hugh** I wish I'd been there to see that. You find anythin?

**Peter** Not much gold. I was too late. Got a wife though.

**Hugh** I've allus been a farmer. And my father and his father before him. Don't know nothin else.

**Peter** My father had a smallholding in Quebec.

**Hugh** You give it up?

**Peter** I'd had enough of the place. It didn't exactly bless me with fortune.

**Hugh** It's good to have a man of your experience around. If there's anythin I can do for ye all's ye have to do is ask.

*Peter hands the mug back to Hugh.*

*The meal.*

**Sarah**
 Broil, bake and boil
 Midday heat
 Sit men table round
 Women dance attendance
 Bow heads
 Father says

50

**Hugh** Let each man give his own thanks in his own way to his own God, whatsoever that may be.

**Sarah**
  Then
  Feed them
  Fill them all up
  With meat and potatoes
  Spread before them
  Best china
  Clink

  *They each raise their glasses. The picture breaks.*

  *Outside the house.*
    *Emer enters and Ruth receives her.*

**Ruth** Sit down, Missus Donaghue and catch your breath.

**Emer** Thank you.

**Ruth** How did you get away over here?

**Emer** I walked.

**Ruth** You must be done out.

**Emer** Not at all.

**Ruth** Why don't you step into the house?

**Emer** I will sit here.

**Ruth** You'd be better off in the shade.

**Emer** I will not go in. Thank you.

**Ruth** Will you take a cup of tea?

**Emer** I have no thirst for tea. How is Sarah?

**Sarah** I'm helpin too.

**Emer** Good for you. The men shouldn't be allowed to think that they do all the work.

**Ruth**  Can I not even get you a wee drink of water?

**Emer**  All right. I'll take a cup of water.

**Ruth**  Right you be . . . Sarah.

*Sarah goes to fetch the water.*
*Silence.*

**Ruth**  So . . . How are you keeping Missus Donaghue?

**Emer**  Well enough.

**Ruth**  Your son and grandson have been very good til us today.

**Emer**  It's a modest wee house, isn't it?

**Ruth**  It does us.

**Emer**  I lived in a shanty much the same myself when first married.

**Ruth**  My husband is talking of a new house.

**Emer**  Men are always starting on one thing before another is finished.

*Peter enters.*

**Peter**  What are you doing here?

*Emer holds out a food parcel and a bottle.*

**Emer**  I brung you this – a bit of bread and cheese and a sup of milk to keep you going.

**Peter**  We have already eaten, Mother.

**Ruth**  Beef and potatoes.

**Peter**  Missus McCrea gave us a good dinner.

**Ruth**  Surely you didn't think I'd let them starve, Missus Donaghue?

**Emer** (*to Peter*) Take it – in case the boy gets hungry later.

**Peter** You'll kill yourself walking about in this heat.

**Emer** I will walk where I want to walk, when I want to walk it.

**Peter** So you will. I'll not be concerned for you more.

**Emer** Nothing to be concerned about.

**Peter** How will you get home?

**Emer** I will sit here and wait till you are done.

**Peter** We'll be a while yet.

*Peter returns to work.*

*The building continues.*

**Sarah**
Rafter by rafter roof goes up
Bang bang goes the hammer
Each nail
A hope
A reason to stay
Sun begins to settle
Meeting land.

**Hugh** It is finished.

**Sarah**
My father says,
And starts his climb
Sure-footed on shaky ladder
To the top
The very top
Of the barn

**Hugh** Hello, Sarah!

**Sarah** Hello!

**Hugh** What a view!

**Sarah** What can you see?

**Hugh** The whole world! I believe I can see the whole world all the way back to Antrim. (*He waves.*) Afternoon, brother Henry! How ye doin? . . . I'm glad to hear it . . . Me? Oh, I'm just dandy now. Can't complain . . . The farm? Four times the size of your holdin and my barn's ten times the size of your'n!

*Ruth enters, her hands cupped as if she is holding a jug.*

**Ruth** Get down from there before you fall and kill yourself, you old fool!

**Hugh** What d'ye think, wife?

**Ruth** That you'll fall and kill yourself.

**Hugh** The barn?! The barn?!

**Ruth** As good as any I've seen.

**Hugh** Better, I think.

**Emer** It's still only firewood – not a treasure house yet.

**Peter** Mother!

**Ruth** Are you thirsty?

**Hugh** I could drink a river.

**Ruth** Lemonade's all I have.

**Hugh** That'll do.

**Ruth** Come down and get it then. There's enough refreshment here for you and the men. Sarah will pour it out for you. (*She hands the 'jug' to Sarah.*) Don't spill it now. There's just enough.

**Sarah** Yes, Ma.

**Ruth** Bring it back when you are done.

*Ruth exits. Michael and Sarah alone.*

**Michael** Look at you! A proper little Felimidh's wife. Dance with me, Ethne! (*He begins to dance with her.*)

**Sarah** Michael, mind!

**Michael** Passing through the great hall, Ethne danced with each of the warriors . . .

*The jug falls and shatters.*

**Sarah** Oh God! Oh my God! It's broke.

**Michael** It's only an old jug.

**Sarah** Did anybody see?

**Michael** I dunno.

**Sarah** So stupid! What am I goin to do?

**Michael** You can make more lemonade.

**Sarah** No! . . . Quick! Pick the pieces up.

**Michael** Sarah, it's only a jug.

*Sarah, distressed, tries to pick up the pieces.*
*Ruth enters.*
*Silence.*

**Sarah** I'm sorry.

**Ruth** I told you to be careful.

**Sarah** I know my granny gave it to you.

**Michael** It was my fault, Missus McCrea . . .

**Sarah** It just fell out of my hand.

**Michael**  I was messing about and I knocked into her . . .

**Sarah**  I'm really sorry, Ma.

**Michael**  I'll pay for it.

**Ruth**  (*to Michael*) Have you no work to do?

  *Michael exits.*

**Sarah**  I'm really, really, sorry.

**Ruth**  All right. Don't make a song and a dance out of it.

**Sarah**  Maybe my granny'll send you a new one if you ask her.

**Ruth**  I carried it with me the whole way here.

**Sarah**  Maybe we can stick it back together?

**Ruth**  It won't be fixed now.

**Sarah**  I can try.

**Ruth**  No. It's broken . . . Let it alone.


### ELEVEN

*Hugh sowing seed. Music.*

**Sarah**
  Spring
  Year of our Lord
  Nineteen hundred and sixteen
  Arctic blast cold chill from the north
  The ploughing begins
  And
  Father scatters seeds in the big pasture
  Good grass sown from the seeds of home
  And it grows

Letter from home tells
More warriors in battle
Red Hand defending Ulster
Green Hand defending Ireland
Rise up all
Defending
Heritage.

## TWELVE

*June 1916. The pasture by the water. Michael reads from a copy of 'The Worker's Republic' newspaper. Sarah enters.*

**Sarah** Hey boy! What're you doin?

**Michael** I thought you were my father.

**Sarah** Skivin are ye?

**Michael** Taking a break.

**Sarah** I went up to the house. Your granny says to give you this.

*She hands him a bottle of milk from which he drinks.*

**Michael** Thanks.

**Sarah** What're you doin out diggin on a Sunday?

**Michael** Peter says we're behind on the sowing.

**Sarah** Remember the Sabbath day to sanctify it.

**Michael** Honour thy father and thy mother that thy days may be long upon the earth which the Lord thy God giveth thee. I know my commandments as well as you.

**Sarah** You might make a priest, but you'll never make a farmer.

**Michael** Good! If I have to stay here the rest of my life I'll go mad.

**Sarah** Where else would you go?

**Michael** Toronto or maybe St John. They're building three factories a day in the East.

**Sarah** You can go only if you promise to take me with you.

**Michael** It is my *geis*.

**Sarah** For I have no desire to marry Robert Milling and spend the rest of my days wedded to my cousin.

**Michael** I hate him.

**Sarah** You hardly even know him . . . He's asked my da to start courtin me as soon as I'm sixteen.

**Michael** What do you say?

**Sarah** I say no.

**Michael** He's a good catch for a girl like you.

**Sarah** What do you mean, 'a girl like me'?

**Michael** He's gonna be a lawyer. You could live in a big house in the city, have fancy clothes and a motor car.

**Sarah** I don't want a motor car.

**Michael** Don't have one then.

**Sarah** And I don't want Robert Milling.

**Michael** Then don't have him either.

> *Silence.*
> *Sarah picks up the newspaper and begins to read.*

**Sarah** 'We must accustom ourselves to the notion of arms, to the use of arms. Bloodshed is a cleansing and sanctifying thing, and the nation which regards it as the final horror has lost its manhood.'

**Michael** Isn't it marvellous?

**Sarah** Isn't it marvellous? No. It's a load of old horse manure if ever I heard one.

**Michael** You can't say that!

**Sarah** I'll say it again if you like. Patrick Pearse is talkin a load of old horse . . . /

**Michael** / . . . Give it back!

**Sarah** No.

**Michael** It's mine.

**Sarah** It should be torn up into squares for the outhouse.

**Michael** Give it back now!

**Sarah** Come and get it.

**Michael** You're being a child, Sarah.

**Sarah** Oh, who's the big man now? Have it back. I don't want it.

**Michael** Thank you.

**Sarah** Thank you.

**Michael** Stop it!

**Sarah** Stop it!

   *A beat.*

**Michael** This is about freedom. You wouldn't understand.

**Sarah** Then don't talk to me any more.

**Michael** I'm an Irishman.

**Sarah** You're as Irish as the grass in the big pasture – the seed may have come from Ireland but the soil it grows in and the rain that waters it is Canadian.

**Michael** I know more of Irish history than you do.

**Sarah** I was born there.

**Michael** I speak Irish.

**Sarah** I was born there.

**Michael** You don't have to be born in a country to belong to it.

**Sarah** Your father says you're a Canadian and he should know.

**Michael** Each generation for the past three hundred years has risen up to free our land of the British. It's tradition.

**Sarah** It's murder. Another commandment broken.

**Michael** Your lot started it all, bringing guns in and killing Catholics in their beds at night.

**Sarah** My lot?

**Michael** I'm sorry.

**Sarah** Leave me alone.

**Michael** Come on.

**Sarah** Get away from me, you . . . you . . . Fenian!

**Michael** It's only play.

**Sarah** You can't call it play when you get so worked up about it.

**Michael** Deirdre was raised as Conor commanded. Every day she grew more beautiful as Cathbad had foretold.

**Sarah** I'm not an idiot.

**Michael** One day when it was snowing and cold as cold, Deirdre was watching her foster father preparing a young calf for the table. As he flayed the skin from its carcass, blood flowed out across the frozen snow and a raven circled overhead, ready to drink from the stream.

**Sarah** 'I could love a man like that,' said Deirdre, 'With hair raven black and skin as white as snow and cheeks as red as blood.'

### THIRTEEN

*November 1916. The Donaghue farmstead.*
  *Emer ushers Sarah in from the cold.*

**Emer** Mihal's not here. He's gone to a meeting of the parish men with his father.

**Sarah** May I wait for him?

  *A beat.*

**Emer** Step in and keep the cold out.

  *Emer returns to her sewing. Sarah offers her a cake.*

**Sarah** I brought you this. It's butter-pound.

**Emer** Thank you. We are not big cake eaters in this house. I'm surprised your mother let you out on a night like this.

**Sarah** I'm on my way back from an errand to the Trimbles.

**Emer** She doesn't know that you have come here?

**Sarah** No.

**Emer** Sit by the fire and warm yourself.

**Sarah** Thank you.

**Emer** You shouldn't walk the roads in such snow.

**Sarah** I told Mike I would come. He said he'd teach me the set dancing.

**Emer** What would you be wanting to learn all that for?

**Sarah** He thinks I should know it. What do you make?

**Emer** Nothing in particular. I sew for its own sake.

**Sarah** It's beautiful.

**Emer** It's a pretty pattern.

**Sarah** I'm a terrible needle-worker. My mother says I've a hand like a foot.

**Emer** It's the eye that's important. As long as you can see, you can sew.

**Sarah** Then I must be blind too.

**Emer** Here. (*She hands Sarah the cloth.*)

**Sarah** I'll ruin it.

**Emer** No matter, it's only cotton. It can be ripped out and started over again.

**Sarah** What do I do?

**Emer** Hold the needle like so.

**Sarah** That's not the proper way.

**Emer** There is no proper way. Only what's comfortable. Is that better? Follow this line here . . . . That's it . . . Now, turn the stitch like so . . . Ah! . . . (*She demonstrates.*) A little too big. See? Like this.

**Sarah** I'm no good at all.

**Emer** All it takes is a bit of practice. Keep on with it. (*She hands Sarah back the needle.*)

**Emer** How is your mother?

**Sarah** Well, thank you. Though she always gets sick for home comin into the winter.

**Emer** I've been here twenty years and I still sicken for it.

**Sarah** Why did you not go back?

**Emer** I met my husband – a good Irishman – and he wanted to stay. We cleared our land, raised our children. There was nothing left to go back for.

**Sarah** Except to see it again.

**Emer** Here. Give me your hand. The one on which you will wear your wedding ring . . . We used to do this when I was a girl. It tells your fortune. Put your hand out flat.

> *Emer rubs the needle three times against the side of Sarah's hand then lets it dangle over the centre of her palm.*

**Sarah** It circles.

**Emer** That means you will have a boy. And again. (*She repeats the process.*)

**Sarah** Another boy.

**Emer** Two sons is a good start. (*And a third time.*) It swings. That's a girl. It's good to have one girl. (*She repeats. This time the needle is still.*) No. No more. Oh well, two boys and a girl is not bad at all.

> *Peter and Michael enter.*

**Sarah** Good evening.

**Peter** What are you doin out on a night like this?

**Sarah** I came to have my dancing lesson.

**Michael** Sorry we're late.

**Peter** Dancing is it?

**Michael** I'm gonna teach Sarah the set dancing.

**Emer** I don't see what she needs to know all that for.

**Peter** No better way to keep warm. (*to Sarah*) Have you been made welcome?

**Emer** Of course she has. Do you think me unmannerly? I will make the tea.

**Sarah** I brought you a cake.

**Michael** Thank you. May I eat it now?

**Emer** There's plenty here for you to eat.

**Sarah** Your granny was tellin my fortune with the sewin needle. I'll have two boys and a girl, she says.

**Michael** They will be well provided for with a lawyer for a father.

**Emer** What's the news?

**Michael** Conscription! All the talk is of conscription. If it comes to it, I'll not go.

**Peter** Easy. It hasn't happened yet. But you should've heard them flapping and quacking away like ducks as usual!

**Michael** Better to be quacking now than shot in the head later.

**Peter** Better a clear and reasoned head, Michael. (*to Sarah*) What do you think?

**Sarah** Of conscription?

**Peter** That's what I asked you.

**Sarah** They need soldiers.

**Peter** Would you go?

**Sarah** I can't.

**Michael** Dad . . . /

**Peter** / . . . Imagine.

**Sarah** I wouldn't.

**Peter** Why not?

**Sarah** Well, I don't understand it all, but . . . /

**Peter** / . . . Good answer.

**Michael** Give me your coat.

*Peter moves Emer's chair.*

**Peter** We'd better clear the floor if we are to have dancing.

**Emer** I don't see the call for all this fuss.

**Peter** If he is to teach her then he must teach her properly.

**Michael** Right. I'll show you. Pretend we're standing in a circle. You're opposite me like this. Now, I'll show you the basic steps. (*slowly*) And one and two and three and cut and back and back and one, two, three, four . . . See? . . . Now you dance to me.

*Sarah makes an attempt.*

**Michael** No. Come down on your heel at the last like this.

**Sarah** I'm no good at all.

**Michael** It's easy once you practise. I'll do it with you.

*He guides and they dance.*

**Peter** And one and two and three and cut . . .

**Emer** I'll show her. It's better a woman shows a woman how to do a woman's steps.

**Michael** No! (*to Sarah*) Now I dance round you . . . And you dance round me.

**Sarah** How am I doing?

**Peter** You've got the spirit of it.

> *Music fades in.*
> *Michael and Sarah take each others hands.*
> *Slowly, they start turning each other.*
> *The dance quickens.*

**Emer** What're you doin, Mihal? . . . Careful!

**Peter** Give them space!

> *Breathless, they stop.*

**Michael** What do you think? Am I a good teacher?

**Sarah** You are.

**Peter** It was fine, wasn't it, Mother?

**Emer** Those weren't the right steps.

**Peter** It's only a start. Only a start.

> *Music.*
> *Sarah and Michael dance, beautifully, fluidly together.*
> *Blackout.*

# Act Two

## ONE

*December 1916.*

**Sarah**
   First nip of winter in the air
   Down to the city we go
   To bring in the supplies
   To take John to war
   Quiet under starlight
   We creep
   Out of the house
   Children curled up in arms
   And into the wagon
   Horses clipclop on heavy earth
   Passing by
   Sod huts of the Doukhobours
   Passing through
   At six road ends
   Township of Stanley
   Lot 42
   Grist mill
   Saw mill
   Merchant shop
   Two churches
   Schoolhouse
   Orange Hall
   Passing through
   Passing along
   Long deserted roads that will soon be flowing rivers
       of mud
   Then frozen under snow.

Knife wind cuts through on the plains
Stretching out on all sides
Ocean of land
Morning wakes up
Before us lies
City on the horizon
Queen of the Plains
Regina
Capital of our province.
Slowly we haul into
Huge and heaving mess
Of mills
Factories
Shop fronts just opening up.

Big engine belching steam
Green carriage new and shiny
Not to carry our cheap cheap wheat
But our men.

Whistle blasts
One two
One two
And he is gone
My brother John
Not yet seventeen years
Off to fight the enemy
Sixty thousand miles away.

### TWO

*December 1916. Department store, Regina.*
   *Ruth and Sarah are buying cloth. Above a sign reads,*
*'No Ruthenians employed here.'*

**Sarah**  He'll be all right, Ma.

**Ruth** Do you think so?

**Sarah** Look how happy he was gettin on the train – he was dead proud of himself.

**Ruth** Pride'll be no shield to him. I wonder at your father letting him go like that.

**Sarah** Ma, he wanted to go.

**Ruth** Thousands of them dead already.

**Sarah** Our John'll not let anybody kill him. He told me he was comin back with a German's helmet as a souvenir.

**Ruth** Have you all the bags?

**Sarah** Aye.

**Ruth** . . . Shoes . . . shirts . . . .

**Sarah** What does that sign mean?

**Ruth** It's to discourage the immigrants seeking work. How many boxes of that liquorice did you lift?

**Sarah** Two.

**Ruth** I said three. We'll have to go back to the confectioner's.

**Sarah** Why don't they want them?

**Ruth** Because there's too many of them and they've no English. Now, material for the winter dresses.

**Sarah** How much do we need?

**Ruth** Let's see. You and I are of a size. I'd say that's twenty yards. Mind now, we only have fifteen dollars to spend.

**Sarah** But my Daddy give you near sixty dollars.

**Ruth** Shh! Do you want everybody to hear?

**Sarah** How about this one?

**Ruth** Too gaudy.

**Sarah** This one?

*Emer enters, unnoticed by Ruth.*

**Ruth** Too expensive. This one here is good, but not so warm. Oh, well. We'll just have to wear extra layers. If only you were able to help me, but you're like a spider weaving its web with a needle in your hand.

**Emer** Hello, Sarah.

**Ruth** Missus Donaghue.

**Emer** Missus McCrea. I see we all have the same idea today.

**Ruth** It's that time of year.

**Emer** Now that is a pretty fabric.

**Ruth** I was just saying that.

**Emer** Poor quality though. But sure, when you haven't much you must make it go further.

**Ruth** Isn't that so. Sarah, we'll take the velveteen.

**Sarah** I though it was too expensive.

**Ruth** Not at all! It'll be far warmer to wear. This one's more a spring fabric – I told you that. We'll take that one.

**Emer** 'Tis a lovely job of work, dress-making. I had no daughters to sew pretty dresses for. No granddaughters neither. Only big strapping boys in our stock. Ye have no sons yourself?

**Ruth** Four, as you know. The oldest, John, is just left for the war.

**Emer** That must distress you sorely.

**Ruth** He goes to do his duty. So we must be proud of him. I wonder at your grandson's not going.

**Emer** I do not . . . Now, this here is a fine material. Good heavy winter cloth. Only two dollars a yard. I think I shall have myself twenty yards of it. Good day to you, Missus McCrea.

**Ruth** Good day.

**Emer** Good day, Sarah. I'll be seeing you again soon, no doubt. (*to Ruth*) Your daughter and my grandson, Mihal, are friendly, you know.

**Ruth** They are acquainted, I believe.

**Emer** Oh, not just acquainted, but thick – very thick. We can't keep them apart. Good day again.

> *Emer exits.*
> *A beat.*

**Ruth** You go up to that woman's house?

**Sarah** I've been there.

**Ruth** Often?

**Sarah** Several times.

**Ruth** What would your father say if he knew?

**Sarah** Where's the harm in it?

**Ruth** Harm?! (*more quietly*) Making love to a . . .

> *A beat.*

**Sarah** I'm making love to nobody.

**Ruth** Your father a leading member of the Order.

**Sarah** I know that.

**Ruth**  With a . . . for a son-in-law! What are you thinking of?

**Sarah**  Mother, people will hear you.

**Ruth**  Don't tell me to be quiet!

**Sarah**  I didn't.

**Ruth**  This would never happen at home. Your grandfather wouldn't let the like of this go on, I'm telling you.

**Sarah**  Are we takin that there material or this one?

**Ruth**  You would know all about it if your grandfather were here.

**Sarah**  For God's sake, Ma . . .

**Ruth**  You thank heaven we are in a public place . . . Never swear at me!

**Sarah**  All right.

**Ruth**  And never – ever – go there again. Do you hear me? There's an end to it.


### THREE

*June 1918. The pasture.*

**Sarah**
    Spring nineteen hundred and eighteen
    Awakens us out of frozen sleep.
    America turns its hand
    To a different plough
    War machine
    To dig it up
    Plough it up
    Churn it up

Europe
More guns
More mines
More dead
All along the Western Front
Boom boom
Boom boom

*Wheat fields on the boundary between the Donaghue
and McCrea farmsteads.*
*Peter and Hugh enter.*

**Peter** It was a hard frost last night.

**Hugh** Very hard for June.

**Peter** You're planted early.

**Hugh** At Easter.

**Peter** I wait until these few trees are in full leaf. The
spring warmth is deceptive.

**Hugh** There's some damage done, I think.

**Peter** It usually comes about now. Think you've got a
good crop and then it's gone.

**Hugh** The weather here is surely differ'nt to home.

**Peter** May I take a look. (*Peter examines a head of
grain.*)

**Peter** Red Fife.

**Hugh** I suppose you planted Marquis?

**Peter** It withstands the frost better. Gives a better yield.

**Hugh** Everybody's all Marquis wheat these days.

**Peter** It's hard to keep up.

**Hugh** Oh, I keep up all right. I bought me a new plough
and two horses there a month or so back.

**Peter**  On loan?

**Hugh**  Aye, but I have doubled my acreage this year.

**Peter**  I got a new seeder.

**Hugh**  On loan?

**Peter**  No, bought it outright. The head's glassy, that's a tell-tale sign, and see, there's the white ring circling the stalk.

**Hugh**  It's ruined then?

**Peter**  Maybe. Maybe not.

**Hugh**  We'll pay the note back. We will. If wheat prices continue to hold at the two dollars.

**Peter**  You must strip the heads and quick about it.

**Hugh**  Where do I cut?

**Peter**  At the first joint below the head. See? I'll give you a hand.

**Hugh**  You can spare the time?

**Peter**  I won't finish this today. I seem to have lost my helper again.

**Hugh**  It's hard when they don't take after you.

**Peter**  They must go their own way. You're short-handed yourself.

**Hugh**  I hired me a few men. One from the Ukraine and a Doukhobour boy. I get twice as much work done myself in a day than the two of them together.

**Peter**  They will not play the servant here.

**Hugh**  Bolsheviks – the lot of them! And argue over pay terrible. I miss my John. But we will have him back for harvest if God spares him.

**Peter** You'd word from him, I hear.

**Hugh** Yesterday.

**Peter** Good news that he is safe.

**Hugh** We thought we had lost him. He was wounded at Vimy.

**Peter** That's – honourable.

**Hugh** Aye. He's a brave lad. How is it that your boy doesn't go?

**Peter** He just has his own mind.

**Hugh** His own?

*The pasture. Sarah and Michael lie together.*

**Michael** Naiose and his brothers undertook brave missions for the Scottish king.

**Sarah** Deirdre kept a veil over her face at all times, lest the king see how beautiful she was.

**Michael** And the king wondered what lay behind the veil.

**Sarah** One morning, before the day had woken up, the king's steward stole into the brother's encampment. Coming upon the lovers asleep in an embrace . . .

**Michael** His eyes fell upon the face of Deirdre and he wept, so beautiful was she. 'Most beautiful lady, the King of Scotland loves you. He asks you to leave this warrior and come to be his wife.'

**Sarah** 'I will not go with you,' she said. 'For I am promised to another.'

**Michael** Close your eyes.

**Sarah** Why?

**Michael**  Just do it.

*He presses a strawberry to her lips. She bites into it.*

**Sarah**  Strawberries!

**Michael**  I grew them myself.

**Sarah**  I thought the frost had killed them all.

**Michael**  Not these ones. Are they sweet?

**Sarah**  No. But not bitter neither. Taste.

*Michael kisses her.*

*Wheat fields on the boundary between the Donaghue and McCrea farmsteads.*
*Peter and Hugh working.*

**Peter**  How much is rotted?

**Hugh**  About half.

**Peter**  I'm sorry.

*A beat.*

**Hugh**  Those boys over in Winnipeg have it all sewn up.

**Peter**  We must stick together. I wonder that you don't join the League of Farmers.

**Hugh**  We never had such things in Antrim. Sure we had meetings, but not organised demonstrations

**Peter**  And that's why you're farming wheat in Canada now instead of flax back home.

**Hugh**  It smacks of socialism to me.

**Peter**  What else are we to do? This government's sympathy lies not in people, but in profit.

**Hugh**  We must all get behind the war effort. That's what I told our John.

**Peter** If the new settlers want to go, let them go. They are still wedded to the old country.

**Hugh** You don't back the war.

**Peter** Oh, it's not the war that bothers me. Let them fight it – it's a just enough war. It's this conscription business I don't like.

**Hugh** You Catholics is all opposed to it.

*Silence.*

**Peter** Nothing to do with being Catholic. Canada's a nation on her own, free to fight her own wars, not the rest of the world's.

**Hugh** That's Fenian talk where I come from.

**Peter** Where you come from, maybe. Here, it's just progress.

*The pasture. Sarah and Michael lie together.*

**Michael** 'You must leave Naoise and come willingly to the king as his bride or be taken away by force and your lover and his brothers slain.'

**Sarah** 'I will not go with you,' she said. D'you know what would go beautiful with these just now?

**Michael** What?

**Sarah** Silverwoods' ice cream. You ever had it?

**Michael** Not Silverwoods'.

**Sarah** When we first came to Toronto we ate Silverwoods' ice cream.

**Michael** When Naoise returned that night she told him of the King of Scotland's treachery.

**Sarah** We must leave Scotland.

**Michael** So away they fled, fugitives adrift on the sea once more . . . I've never been to Toronto.

**Sarah** Never?

**Michael** Never.

**Sarah** Look at me! I'm covered.

*They kiss.*

**Sarah**
  Little seeds pop pop popping
  Sweet like sugar cane
  Sugar sweet little strawberry kiss
  Flutter-belly
  Like jumpin off high tree into stream.
  Hands grapple my hands
  Arms holdin him
  Fingertips pressing into my shoulder
  Hands on my hands, my legs
  Hands up and under my skirt to my
  Belly.

  So close
  Skin on skin
  His touch
  Feather soft
  Oh, he is beautiful!
  Scent of his hair all meadow-perfume
  Eyelash tickle on my cheek.
  This is not a bad thing.

  I bury myself
  I rise and fall on him
  Like the big ship on the ocean.

  Bad?
  Not bad.
  Not me.
  Never.

Between my legs he rests
And his hair is soft as hay
Like good hay sown from the grass seed
Sent in the crease of the letter from home.
No.

Not home.
This is home.

## FOUR

*June 1918. The McCrea farmstead.*
  *Sarah, Hugh and Ruth.*

**Ruth** What's lost?

**Hugh** All – except forty acres.

**Ruth** What's to be done?

**Hugh** The oats will be all right. We'll have to make oor money ootay those. The buildin of the new hoose will hae to wait a while. (*to Sarah*) You've been goin up to the Donaghue house.

**Sarah** So I have.

**Hugh** Often?

**Sarah** Only once or twice.

**Ruth** Didn't I tell you not to go up there?

**Sarah** You did.

**Ruth** I warned you.

**Hugh** Hush, Ruth. (*to Sarah*) I don't like it that you see Michael Donaghue so much.

**Sarah** I don't see him often.

**Ruth** Yes, you do.

**Sarah** He's a neighbour.

**Hugh** No one's tellin ye not to be neighbourly. Just break the habit of seein him alone.

**Sarah** Why?

**Ruth** Sarah!

**Hugh** No . . . It's a straightforward enough question. (*to Sarah*) I dinnae like his father's politics.

**Sarah** His father never talks about Ireland.

**Hugh** Whatever he thinks about Ireland is his own concern.

**Sarah** Then what is it?

**Hugh** They're republicans, through and through.

**Sarah** They're Canadians.

**Hugh** That's the same thing in my book.

**Sarah** No it's not.

**Hugh** Are you contradictin me? . . . I'll have nae truck with republicans.

   *A beat.*

**Sarah** All I'm sayin is, Da, this here's a new country. You're always tellin us that.

**Hugh** There's some things that shouldnae be forgot.

**Sarah** More that shouldnae be remembered.

**Hugh** Where does she get these notions from?

**Ruth** Where do you think?

**Sarah** I get them from myself.

**Ruth** (*to Hugh*) You've brought it on yourself.

**Hugh** (*to Sarah*) It turns me to think of you with him.

**Sarah** He's my friend.

**Ruth** I hope friends is all it is.

**Hugh** Ruth . . .

**Ruth** Well, is it?

**Sarah** Friends is all.

**Ruth** I've never made friends with a Catholic in my life. Their bigotry is too much.

**Sarah** Michael's people are good, kind people, Ma.

**Hugh** Better see him no more in future.

**Sarah** I can't just stop speakin to him, Daddy!

**Ruth** You'll do as you're told to do.

**Sarah** He's my friend.

**Hugh** All right. Ye've done nae wrong. He's only your friend and that was fine while youse were children, but youse are near grown now. Things is differ'nt when you're grown.

**Sarah** I don't see how.

**Hugh** Because people is all differ'nt! . . . D'ye understand?

**Sarah** I understand.

**Hugh** There now. Ye willnae see him again, sure ye won't?

**Sarah** No.

**Hugh** D'ye promise me?

*Silence.*

See him again and I'll be hard on you. D'ye hear me?

**Sarah**  I hear.

**Hugh**  Come on! There's plenty more young men to take your fancy, eh? There's young Robert Milling, soon to be a lawyer like his father and his grandfather before him. He still pays you attention.

**Sarah**  I thought it was unnatural to marry a cousin.

**Ruth**  It could be worse.


FIVE

*Autumn 1918.*

**Sarah**
    Fall
    Leaves on gold fields
    War no more
    Germany
    Turkey
    Austria
    All fall down
    Bow to righteous Empire
    No more
    Boom boom
    Armistice
    End.

*Ruth enters, with a sheet in her arms. She rocks her son, John, to sleep.*

Half come home of those who went
And some of they are only half of what they were
Brother John returns

But not to harvest
Hollow as reed
Pale as milk
All a-tremble
Screamin terror
Sweat-lashin
She rock-a-byeing him in her arms
Sayin –

**Ruth** There, there, my son. You're all right now. You're home.


### SIX

*November 1918.*
*The pasture by the water.*

**Sarah** He saw men lyin dead.

**Michael** And killed too.

**Sarah** I expect so. He won't say more about it.

**Michael** Things can start moving in Ireland again. There'll be elections for the new parliament next month. We'll be a republic before Christmas.

**Sarah** Don't talk to me about that. It's all anyone can speak of now – you, my father . . .

**Michael** Where'd you say you'd gone?

**Sarah** Into Stanley for cotton.

**Michael** That's not a good lie.

**Sarah** They'd never think I'd lie to them so one lie's as good as another.

**Michael** I don't like sneaking about like a criminal.

**Sarah** Then don't come and meet me any more.

**Michael** Take your hair down. I like the look of it that way.

**Sarah** . . . Look above. What a sight!

**Michael** Sharp-shins going south. All the way down to Florida.

**Sarah** There's thousands of them.

**Michael** They're flying high.

**Sarah** Means a hard winter.

**Michael** Wouldn't you just love to be away up there with them?

**Sarah** Why don't we go?

**Michael** Where?

**Sarah** Toronto – like you said.

**Michael** I'd go to the United States. There's farms to be had out west.

**Sarah** Think again. You're no farmer.

**Michael** Toronto it is, then.

**Sarah** When'll we go?

**Michael** In the springtime, after the planting.

**Sarah** Why not today?

**Michael** Today it is then.

**Sarah** What'll we do there?

**Michael** Go to Silverwoods' dairy.

**Sarah** We could get married.

**Michael** What do you mean?

**Sarah** What I said.

**Michael** We can't do that.

**Sarah**  Who says?

**Michael**  If we don't pray in the same church together we can't marry.

**Sarah**  I think we've done worse than pray together, Mike.

**Michael**  I know that.

**Sarah**  So I'm to give you all this for nothing?

**Michael**  It's not for nothing, I hope.

**Sarah**  You tell me. All's I know is I have given you all of me . . . Do you love me?

**Michael**  Sarah . . .

**Sarah**  Tell me.

**Michael**  Yes.

**Sarah**  Say it. (*A beat.*) What's the matter? I can say it. I love Michael Donaghue! I'd tell anybody.

**Michael**  *Taím i ngrá leat.*[19]

**Sarah**  In English.

**Michael**  I love you. Now you say it in Irish.

**Sarah**  *Taím i ngrá leat.*

**Michael**  That's terrible!

**Sarah**  To hell with the Pope!

**Michael**  Shh! Sarah, don't say that.

**Sarah**  Why not? He can't hear me.

**Michael**  You're a rebel, d'you know that? You're a hardened revolutionary, Sarah McCrea.

---

[19] I love you.

85

*Spring 1919.*
  *The McCrea farmstead.*
  *Hugh and Ruth wait. Sarah enters.*

**Hugh**  So, you're returned.

**Sarah**  I am.

**Hugh**  Where'd ye go?

**Sarah**  Out walking across the fields.

**Hugh**  On your own?

**Sarah**  You know I wasn't. She saw me.

**Ruth**  Who do you call 'she'?

**Hugh**  Ah, Sarah, Sarah . . . What did I tell ye?

**Ruth**  Remember what you said, Hugh.

**Hugh**  (*to Sarah*) What possessed you? After all we talked about?

**Ruth**  Hugh . . .

**Hugh**  I know what I said. (*to Sarah*) What did I say til ye?

**Sarah**  That I was to walk out with Michael Donaghue no more.

**Hugh**  But you did so?

**Sarah**  I did.

**Hugh**  Sarah . . .

**Ruth**  Headstrong, she is!

**Hugh**  All right! I'm tryin to talk til her!

**Ruth** Talk til her?! How many times have you talked til her?

**Hugh** Will ye leave it in my hands?

**Ruth** She cannae carry on like this. You're the one said it . . . Soft!

**Hugh** Soft am I, now?

**Ruth** No. Weak. Do you hear me? Weak! You backed up arguing with Henry over your share of the land being willed away to Henry . . . /

**Hugh** / . . . Don't start on that again, Missus! My father was dyin.

**Ruth** No matter. You backed up and let the land go, making yourself no better than a hired hand.

**Hugh** Christ, ye have to go back years!

**Ruth** Don't curse!

**Hugh** Ye allus have to go back years, every bloody difference we have!

**Ruth** Bringing us away out here to make a something out of nothing.

**Hugh** To make us a fortune.

**Ruth** To live in a sod hut, break our backs and lose a child! And not a word have I ever spoken . . . /

**Hugh** / . . . You say plenty. In words and in looks – always downin me.

**Ruth** I only ever worked to raise you up.

**Hugh** Shut your mouth now!

**Ruth** I tell you this and I tell you no more: you give in to this one here tonight and you'll surely have a Fenian

87

for a son-in-law. Now either you do what you said you would or I'll do it myself.

> *Silence.*
>> *Hugh undoes his belt.*
>> *Music.*

**Hugh** (*to Sarah*) Come here to me, you.

**Sarah**
> He says.
> But it is he who moves towards me.
> And I look into my father's eyes
> I want to say,
> 'No, Daddy. Don't beat me and I will never see him
>> again.'
> But the words do not come
> They cannot.
> A draft creeps in under the door, around my ankles
>> and up under my skirt.
> I say to myself
> It is *his* touch
> In the big pasture
> When I ate strawberries and kissed him
> My mouth full of the sweet taste.
> He grasps the belt
> I hear her draw breath.

**Ruth** Now you'll listen.

**Sarah**
> She says.
> First crack of pain
> Flying forwards
> Left arm across my chest
> Winded
> Flying backwards
> Slam onto table
> I close my eyes

I make no sound
He is breathing hard
Second, third, fourth crack come down across my spine
He stops
After each blow
Waiting
For a tear, a plea, a cry
I give him nothing.

**Ruth** Enough now.

**Sarah**
I hear buckle clunk on floor
He grabs me by shoulders
Throws me backwards
We are dancing
And one and two and three and cut
Hitting me now with hand open
Bang on this side of the head
Bang on the other
Round and round we go

**Ruth** Enough now. Hugh!

**Sarah**
Against the wall
Against the door
Against the floor
Under table
Tumbling on back
Feet chase me to the other side
Hands drag me up again
And bang on this side of the head
And bang on the other
And bang in the face
Mouth fills with thick salt taste.
She is screaming now

**Ruth** Stop! Stop!

**Sarah**
And back and back and fall to the floor . . .
It is cold
Soothing
The little ones are at the doorway
I can hear them
Cryin.

*Ruth shouts to the children offstage.*

**Ruth** Go up to bed now, the lot of you. Upstairs this minute or I'll give youse all something to cry about. (*She crosses to Sarah.*) Sit up.

**Hugh** You don't see him no more.

*Silence.*

**Ruth** Sarah?

**Hugh** D'ye hear me?!

**Ruth** She hears you. She hears you.

*Sarah remains lying on the floor.*


EIGHT

*Spring 1919. Donaghue farmstead.*

**Peter** A man maybe he goes exploring. He comes across something good, rich – a big diamond ring, say. 'I'll have that for myself,' he says. Now what do we call that?

**Michael** I'm late already.

**Peter** Then be late. When it comes to a good piece of land, we call that pioneering. Now this pioneer gets caught red-handed by the man was there before him – the owner. But our pioneer y'see, he doesn't want to back off, so he fights the owner, beats him back or kills him.

**Emer** How's Sarah?

**Michael** I don't know.

**Peter** Finally, our pioneer, he looks at this beautiful gold ring and he thinks to himself, 'What use is the ring to me like this?' So he melts it down, breaks the big stone into little pieces, sells it off and makes a profit.

**Emer** (*to Michael*) Have you had a falling out?

**Michael** No.

**Peter** Now the previous owner might see that as destruction . . .

**Emer** (*to Michael*) That's good.

**Peter** . . . but to the settler that's progress.

**Michael** And that's what happened in Ireland.

**Peter** And what are we doing here except farming land that never belonged to us?

**Emer** It's not the same thing at all, Peadar.

**Michael** This country belonged to land agents.

**Peter** And before them?

**Michael** You didn't fight the Indians for the farm, Peter.

**Peter** No. The French took the land from the Indians and then the English took it from the French. There were a few Dutch mixed up in it somewhere, too. Whichever way you look at it, I bought a little piece of the diamond. So what do you want to do, Mike? After I'm dead, you want to trek up north to the reservation, find the big chief and give him the deed to the farm?

**Michael** No

**Peter** No?

**Michael** All right then, yes! Yes I do.

**Peter** Good for you! That's integrity. But which one of the Plains owns it? The Metis, or is it the Cree or the Alongquipin?

**Michael** I'll give it to them that originally owned it.

**Peter** They all owned it one time or another. Be careful what you're getting into, Michael.

**Emer** It's only meetings. (*to Michael*) Go on now.

**Peter** I've heard whispers that there's more planned than talk.

**Michael** What've you heard?

**Peter** That they've been burning barns over near Hamilton.

**Emer** He'd never get mixed up in all that.

**Michael** That was in retaliation for –

**Peter** If you're going to fight, do it out in the open.

**Michael** For an attack on a Catholic farmer's livestock by a group of Loyalists.

**Peter** None of this jumping about in shadows.

**Michael** You're sounding like McCrea.

**Peter** We don't disagree on everything.

**Michael** He beats her.

**Emer** For friendship with you?

**Michael** He tells her that if I go there, she will suffer for it.

**Peter** That's hard.

**Michael** What do I do about that then, father?

**Emer** Just what you are doing – let it go.

**Michael** Tell me, honest.

**Peter** Is she a good girl, Michael?

**Michael** I believe it.

**Peter** Does she believe the same of you?

**Michael** More than I believe of myself.

**Peter** Then if you want her, take her to you and let no one come between.

*Michael crosses to where Sarah lies on the floor, picks her up and holds her.*


NINE

*Autumn 1919.*

**Sarah**
Day to day
Small army marches farm to farm
Harvesting
They come
Bagging-hook and basket armed
Under blue so big
Hazy heat broods over
Red wheat splashed white with barley
All hands to
Reap and bind and bale
Scalded green lies the plain
Fruits of the earth in their season
Gathered in
Safe in the big barn it lies
And thank we all our God
But we do not live by bread alone
Not us

*The Harvest Fair, township of Stanley.*
  *Sarah joins Ruth at the McCrea barrow.*

**Sarah**
  For now comes
  The fair
  Cold sunshine
  Sweet breeze
  Apples pears plums
  Taties carrots cabbages
  Barrow by barrow
  All in a row
  Our barrow
  Butter and eggs

**Ruth**  Twelve dollars and forty eight-cents.

**Sarah**  Is that all?

**Ruth**  Enough to buy a few bits of groceries for the winter.

**Sarah**
  Swarm
  Stanley
  Six road ends
  Do I hear
  Trading
  Twelve dollars
  Twelve
  Fourteen dollars
  Do I hear
  Fourteen
  Clydesdales
  Apaloosians
  Fourteen
  Ponies
  Steers
  Stallions

Street running
Up and down
Sixteen dollars
Eighteen dollars
Eighteen
Do I hear
Twenty
Twenty dollars
Black stallion
Eighteen hands high
Rearing

*Hugh enters.*

**Ruth** Well?

**Hugh** They're sold.

**Ruth** How much?

**Hugh** Twelve dollars each.

**Ruth** That'll not pay even interest on the note.

**Hugh** Look, Missus I know that, but the two animals was near done out. Donaghue has offered me for the pasture land – six hundred dollars.

**Ruth** We must sell the machinery.

**Hugh** Who'll buy it? Samuel says that he'll make us a loan if we need it.

**Ruth** We cannot take it.

**Hugh** What would you do? Starve.

**Ruth** You've accepted, then? (*to Sarah*) Go and give two pennies each to the boys for spending. Tell them not to be wasting it.

**Hugh** I've told Robert Milling that you'll dance wi' him the night.

**Sarah** Why?

**Hugh** What d'ye mean, why? Because he asked me and I said yes.

**Sarah** I don't want to go to the dance.

**Hugh** Aye, ye do! Girls love the dancing.

**Sarah** Ma?

**Ruth** She's tired, Hugh. We've been working all day.

**Hugh** After all the Millings have done for us?

**Ruth** That doesn't make a match.

**Hugh** (*to Sarah*) In the name of God, just dance wi' the fella.

**Ruth** Let her alone, Hugh.

**Hugh** I've told him now.

**Sarah**
So I walk with him
My cousin
Heavy arm on my shoulders
Organ grinding rusty tune
Round roll-a penny booth
Round merry-go-round
Up and down
Swing boats
Pull on a rope
And up up we go
And down down
Sick I am
His chimney breath
Choking me
I will not dance with you
Says I
You will, says he

And lifts me up
And so it begins
Turning me
Burling me
Round and round
Til I can hardly stand
Never mind
Place one foot in front of the other

*Michael enters.*

**Michael** Enjoying yourself?

**Sarah** Do I look like I'm enjoyin myself?

**Michael** That's a handsome young man you've got there.

**Sarah** He looks like a pig.

**Michael** Now you must have him if Daddy says you must.

**Sarah** I will not have him.

**Michael** I think you will.

**Sarah** Dance with me.

**Michael** No . . . Here?

**Sarah** Yes, here. Why not here?

**Michael** No.

**Sarah** Why not?

**Michael** All right then. When Conor the King heard of the lovers' flight, he said

**Sarah** 'Let them return to Emain Macha.'

**Michael** He sent Fergus, a warrior of honour, and his own son, Cormac, to meet them.

**Sarah** But on the way he laid a trap for them. What's that smell on you?

**Michael** Nothing.

**Sarah** Smoke.

**Michael** We were burning up the chaff yesterday is all.

**Sarah** James Lightbody's hay rick was burned last night.

**Michael** Was it? Conor the King ambushed the lovers and a bloody battle raged.

**Sarah** Naiose was slain but not before he had slit Cormac's throat and killed him.

*Hugh breaks them apart and dances Sarah off.*

**Hugh** Isn't he some dancer now? Shift you! (*to Sarah*) What're you doin? Heh? What?

**Sarah** I'm only dancin.

**Hugh** D'ye know what he is?

**Sarah** No. What is he, Daddy?

**Hugh** Don't try an' make a fool out of me.

**Sarah** I'm not the one doin that.

**Hugh** You will dance with Robert Milling.

**Sarah** I won't.

**Hugh** By Christ, I'll kill ye.

**Michael** Mister McCrea!

**Hugh** Get away from me. Get away and stay away.

**Sarah** Mike . . .

**Hugh** Shut up!

**Michael** I'm telling you, Mister McCrea.

**Hugh** Somebody better go quick and get this wee bastard's da.

**Ruth** Now, Hugh, there's people looking.

**Michael** I'm no bastard.

**Hugh** Aren't ye? That's no' what I heard. I heard your mammy was a travellin stage hoor who'd been tossed by every man up the Klondike.

*Michael goes for Hugh. Peter rushes in and stops him.*

**Peter** Mike!

**Michael** Did you hear what he said?

**Peter** Let him have his opinions. It makes no difference to me.

**Hugh** Right, big man, get this wee fella of yours to hell's gates or I'll send him there myself.

**Peter** Let's go, son.

**Hugh** And keep him away from me and mine.

**Peter** He goes where he wants. I put no rein on him.

**Hugh** Well you tether him or I'll leather him! You, thinkin so much of yersel. So right about all things.

**Michael** Did you hear what he said. Do something!

**Peter** What would you have me do, Mike?

**Michael** Defend us.

**Peter** Against what? Ignorance?

**Hugh** D'ye think? I know all about you. And I'm telling you, I'll not have my line soiled with that.

**Michael** Damn you!

**Ruth** Sarah, come here.

**Emer** Hugh McCrea! Hugh McCrea, take your hands off my grandson . . . There'll be no more of this. (*to Michael*) Get over here now and stand beside me. Sarah, go to your mother.

**Hugh** Keep out of this!

**Emer** I will not.

**Hugh** I do not want to lay eyes on this young Fenian near my daughter in future.

**Emer** If you would listen a moment.

**Hugh** Tell the oul woman to shut up!

**Emer** I'm no oul woman . . .

**Hugh** Look, Missus. This isn't an argument for you.

**Emer** Oh be quiet man, I'm agreeing with ye. I certainly want no more of my blood mixed in with your sort. One of your lot was enough.

**Peter** If you shame me in public, mother . . .

**Emer** You can do that with no help from me, standing there letting this Puritan talk to you like a child. It's the two of you that's at fault. You let it run on too long. Do you see what happens? If I thought a marriage would come out of this . . . *Mharaodh se me. An glsoiseann tú méa, Mhicil?* [20]

**Peter** Don't blackmail him.

**Emer** Do you understand me? I want an end to this business. Here's what will happen. Michael will keep away from Sarah. I will see to it if I have to chain him to my wrist, I'll see to it.

---

[20] It would kill me. Do you hear me, Michael?

**Michael**  Mamo.

**Emer**  I didn't ask you to speak. What a carry on this is!
And if he doesn't keep to it, then we will send him away
to work.

**Peter**  Am I allowed to speak?

**Emer**  Indeed not. Sure what have you ever said that's
any use at all? (*to Hugh and Ruth*) The rest is your
concern. There will be no more lending of tools or
helping hands or even a word spoke between us from
this day on. Fair enough?

**Hugh**  Fair enough.

**Emer**  Good. (*to Sarah*) Now you, go home with your
mother and father and do as they tell you.

> *Sarah exits and Ruth follows her. Emer brandishes her
> walking stick at Hugh.*

That girl you have's a fine, clever, honest, young woman.
And if I hear you've been less than good til her, I'll come
after you and rattle your skull for you, Hugh McCrea.


### TEN

*Spring 1920. Night.
Sarah waits, hidden.
Michael enters.*

**Sarah**  Hey! Donaghue!

**Michael**  Sarah? Where are you?

**Sarah**  Over here . . . You're getting warmer . . . Warmer . . .
Hot . . . Hot . . . Hot!

**Michael**  What are you doin here?

**Sarah**  Aren't you pleased to see me?

**Michael**  Your father'll give you the gears.

**Sarah**  He'll be home late and he'll be full. There's a lodge meeting tonight.

**Michael**  My grandmother'll kill the both of us.

**Sarah**  I had to come . . . What's happened to you?

**Michael**  Nothing.

**Sarah**  Don't give me nothing Mike, you're hurt.

**Michael**  I got into a fight.

**Sarah**  Who with?

**Michael**  Your sweetheart, Robert Milling.

**Sarah**  He's no love of mine.

**Michael**  And John.

**Sarah**  John?

**Michael**  Them and a few others. They sort of bumped into me coming out of the meeting?

**Sarah**  Meeting? Ah, Michael!

**Michael**  Just a meeting. Only a meeting.

**Sarah**  Were they drunk?

**Michael**  Stone, cold sober. 'What sort of meeting's this?' Johnny boy says. So I told him. 'Youse are raisin money to buy guns for murderers,' he says. Then they laid into me – feet and all.

**Sarah**  I'll gut him! I told you nothing good would come of all this Deval, Davel, De Van –

**Michael**  De Valera.

**Sarah** Aye, whatever his name is.

**Michael** You should've seen it, Sarah! One of De Valera's right hand men. He fought right beside James Connolly in the Uprising. He reloaded his gun for him. The room was packed wall to wall. I had to pull myself up onto a table to stop myself getting crushed. You should've heard him! 'Ireland has tirelessly struggled for her freedom since the hour she was first put in chains. Now . . . our day has come at last! A parliament has been set up, the true government of the free nation of Ireland. The organisation of which you are member has set up a committee to arm the Defenders of Ireland. I see young men in this room and it fires my blood. Young exiled sons of Ireland, do not despise your youth. Young comrades in Canada, join us in our struggle . . . ' You're not listening to me.

**Sarah** I am.

**Michael** Sarah, he was right there in the room with me.

**Sarah** He's just a man, Mike, like any other . . . I'm listening.

**Michael** And we all stood up and waved our fists in the air and someone started singing, 'A nation once again, a nation once again! And Ireland long a province be a nation once again.'

**Sarah** My father says the Bolsheviks are taking over the whole world.

**Michael** Loyalist bastard!

**Sarah** Don't call him that.

**Michael** You're defending him?

*A beat.*

**Sarah** Will you come tomorrow to the stream?

**Michael** Sarah . . . /

**Sarah** / . . . Will you come?

**Michael** Yes . . . Go home.


### ELEVEN

*The same night. Outside the Donaghue farmstead.*
*Emer waiting. Peter enters.*

**Peter** Mother, come inside. It's too cold to be standing about.

**Emer** I'm warm enough.

**Peter** The doctor said . . .

**Emer** *A Dhía dhilis!* Only a cough and a splutter.

**Peter** Mother . . .

**Emer** There's nothing to worry about, Peadar.

   *A beat.*

**Peter** I told him to be back here before midnight.

**Emer** He's of age. He can do as he wishes.

**Peter** Where did he go?

**Emer** Into Stanley for a . . . .

**Peter** A meeting! Another meeting. I told him!

**Emer** It's good for him to be interested.

**Peter** In what? Getting himself killed? . . . Joseph Trimble's bull was found lying in a ditch with its throat slit last night.

**Emer** Who'd do a thing like that?

**Peter** And what about these fire-settings?

**Emer** Families feuding . . . /

**Peter** / . . . It frightens me.

**Emer** It's only meetings.

*A silence.*
*Michael enters.*

**Michael** Mamo. You should be in bed.

**Emer** And so should you? Where have you been until this hour of the night?

**Michael** I told you. Into Stanley.

**Emer** You were told to be back before midnight.

**Peter** To do what?

**Michael** To meet with friends. Mamo, I'm a man.

**Peter** We're calling them friends now?

**Emer** You're not so grown yet.

**Peter** I thought we agreed no more meetings?

**Michael** You may have done so.

**Emer** Go to your bed!

**Peter** You know what kind of a district we live in?

**Michael** I won't be ordered to bed, Mamo.

**Emer** Now you listen to me, Mihal . . .

**Peter** Mother, let me talk to him.

**Emer** What's happened to you?

**Michael** I got in a fight coming out of the meeting is all.

**Emer** God in heaven!

**Peter**  Who with?

**Michael**  Some of the lodge men . . . John McCrea.

**Peter**  For God's sake, Michael!

**Michael**  I gave back as good as I got.

**Peter**  And that's what worries me, Michael. That's what worries me.

**Michael**  It's only meetings.

**Emer**  (*to Peter*) It's only meetings.

**Peter**  He doesn't tell me where he goes when he leaves the house any more. He doesn't even lower himself to lie about it. Now . . . Now, this!

**Emer**  That's what happens when you let them run free.

**Peter**  I know the fault lies with me: leaving him to you for all these years to go filling his head with romantic nonsense about the Old Country and coffin ships and martyred rebels. Now he's going to get himself . . . /

**Michael**  / She only told me my history.

**Peter**  That's not history!

**Emer**  What more should I expect from a man who hasn't been to mass this past twenty years?

**Peter**  I will not attend the church that refused to recognise my marriage.

**Emer**  How could it? With all that she was? How could it?

**Peter**  Well, I recognise it and to hell with you and the Pope and anyone else who doesn't!

**Michael**  Leave her alone!

**Emer**  Godless! That's what you are . . .

**Peter** You want him to get himself killed? That's what you want?

**Michael** I won't get myself killed, Peter. Don't you worry about me.

**Peter** Be quiet, boy! Be quiet!

**Emer** Mihal, it is only meetings?

**Peter** Only meetings? (*He pulls Michael by the coat, towards Emer.*) Smell! Smell it?

*Emer smells the coat.*

**Emer** Smoke.

**Michael** I wasn't smoking, Mamo. Honest.

**Peter** You want him to kill himself?

*Emer's coughing fit returns.*

**Peter** Mother . . . I'm sorry . . . Come inside, will you? Come.

**Emer** (*to Michael*) You will not go any more.

**Michael** Mamo . . .

**Emer** You will not go.

**Michael** You can't tell me that.

*Michael exits.*

**Emer** Mihal! I haven't finished yet. Michael! Don't walk away from me. *Mharaodh se me. An glsoiseann tú méa, Mhicil?*[21]

---

[21] It would kill me. Do you hear me, Michael?

## TWELVE

*Spring 1920. Day.*
  *A graveyard. Michael and Peter stand at Emer's graveside.*
  *Sarah enters.*

**Sarah**
  Lord , have mercy.

**Michael**
  Christ, have mercy.

**Sarah**
  Lord, have mercy.
  Ding dong
  Snaky procession black through stones grey
  Open earth
  To swallow it up
  Seed of life
  Departed
  Will not grow again.

**Peter** *and* **Michael**
  Lord Jesus Christ
  Deliver souls of all faithful
  From pains of hell and deep pit

**Sarah**
  Mumble word jumble
  This is the sign of the cross

**Sarah, Peter** *and* **Michael**
  Amen.

**Sarah**
  Silent staring stands he
  Through fingers running memory dust

**Peter**
May hell not swallow up
Nor may they fall into darkness

**Sarah**
Shovel it all in
Dirt

**Peter**
Eternal light shine upon her
Holy light once promised to Abraham and his seed

**Sarah**
Slap backslap
Shake handshake

**Michael**
Eternal rest grant her
With your saints
Forever.
For you are Merciful, O Lord.

**Sarah**
Bye.
Goodbye.

*Peter exits.*
*Sarah approaches Michael.*

**Sarah** Is it all right that I came? . . . Where's your father gone?

**Michael** To start the planting . . . Someone will see you.

**Sarah** . . . For a full year, Deirdre did not smile or speak or lift her head to look upon the faces of those who had killed her beloved. Her heart was broken and nothing would mend it . . .

**Michael** We killed her.

**Sarah** It was the influenza, Mike.

**Michael** Go home.

**Sarah** Conor the King sent Deidre away to dwell with the evil . . . /

**Michael** / . . . Stop!

**Sarah** On the way she hurled her body from the chariot into the way of a huge boulder and was slain . . . Finish it.

**Michael** You know the ending.

   *Silence.*

The true friends of Deidre and Naoise claimed her body and gently laid it in the earth next to her lover. In time . . . In time . . .

**Sarah** I can't stay here . . . Come away with me, Michael.

**Michael** I have work to do here.

**Sarah** What work? . . . It's finished, Michael . . . In time two yew trees grew up from out of their graves and did not cease to grow until their branches entwined.

**Michael** You can't go without me.

**Sarah** Then I will go with you.

   *Silence.*

**Michael** I love you.

**Sarah** Where?

**Michael** Toronto . . . When?

**Sarah** Tonight.

**Michael** Not tonight.

**Sarah** Why not? . . . When?

**Michael** I will come for you. Tonight. I will come for you tonight. I promise.


THIRTEEN

*Spring 1920. Night.*
  *The McCrea farmstead.*

**Sarah**
  I lay sleep-drifting, dreaming of
  Toronto-we-will-go
  And calico
  And Silverwoods' ice cream.
  He comes calling up at my window

**Michael** I have come, true to my *geis* –

**Sarah**
  He says.
  We strawberry kiss and I says, he says . . .
  Strange scent
  Oven bread
  Who would be baking bread this time of night?
  Sleep
  Silverwoods' dairy . . .

**Michael** Sarah!

**Sarah**
  I am sure.
  Calling
  Under my window

**Michael** Come!

**Sarah**
  Crystal clear.
  I come . . .
  Quiet.

111

Too quiet.
No dog-bark.
Through night eyes
I see
Shadows moving in shadows
Men of the night: masked men.
Light at the window
Bright not moonlight
Orange
It is old but it is beautiful . . .
Crash of glass smash on wood.

**Hugh** Jaysus!

**Sarah**
Rattle, rattle, rattle, bedsprings
Thud trip bang bang

**Ruth** What's there?! Who?!

**Sarah**
Smell of
Bread burning
Smell of

**Hugh** Fire! Fire in the barn! Fire!

**Sarah**
Awake I am and
Running
Out into the nightmen night
Frozen I
Eyes on fire
I see
Our barn roaring flames
Doorposts of my brother's burning
Rafters of the lodgemen snapping
Little shingle where my nail went in
Crashing down into

Burning, popping grain.
I see
Mother father oh mammydaddy water dancing

**Peter** And one and two and three

*Michael appears, dancing to the beat of a drum.*

**Sarah**
And splash
And back and back
And one, two, three, four
I hear
Singing
A man singing.
Is he?
No screaming
I see
In the fire
Man
Orange man
Leaping
Flinging arms updown
Crackle crackle crackle jig
I know who he
Can't be –
Smell of smoke on topcoat
Can't be –
Sweet strawberry juice on my lips
Toronto and Silverwoods' ice cream
Splash him down
Oh mammydaddy
No
Please God
No
Hands grasp shoulders hurling me back
No
I will go forward

Break through hands
To see
I see
Black burning skin like potato leaves
Crumble into ashes

**Emer** That destroyed Ireland –

**Sarah**
His granny said.
Hands white
Waxy white mash melting
Under red burned blood
Charred all through to the bone
Feet still jig-dancing
Muscle blackened meat, all spoiled.
His hair
Sour smoke rising
His no lips gasping fear-wide eyes.

*Hugh tries to douse the flames with a blanket.*

**Hugh** Come on boy, breathe!

**Sarah** No.

**Hugh** Don't look at him.

**Ruth** Sarah, come away with me into the house.

**Sarah**
Come back to me.
Dance! D'ye hear me?
Get up to your feet and dance!

## FOURTEEN

*After the fire. The McCrea farmstead.*
  *Ruth tries to comfort Sarah.*

**Hugh** (*to Sarah*) He wasn't on his own. I saw two or three more runnin away. D'ye know who it was?

**Ruth** How's she going to know that?

**Hugh** Well, she knew him didn't she? She knew him. (*to Sarah*) Will you answer me?

**Ruth** Leave her in peace, Hugh.

**Hugh** No one ever razed a barn so quick as that.

**Ruth** We can build another barn.

**Hugh** With what? Ashes?

**Ruth** (*to Sarah*) You'll be all right.

**Hugh** Everything I have. My whole. And she sits there and will not speak to me.

**Ruth** Leave her alone. (*to Sarah*) What're you crying for?

**Hugh** She's cryin for him.

  *Ruth faces Hugh.*

**Ruth** Leave her alone now, I tell you. (*to Sarah*) There now. You'll be all right . . . I know . . . The Lord is my shepherd, I shall not want. He maketh me to lie down in green pastures . . .

**Sarah** No more.

**Ruth** He leadeth me beside the still waters . . .

**Sarah**
Mine
Black ashes
All mine
Shouldn't be forgotten
None can redeem

**Ruth**  I know . . .

**Sarah**
Dubadum
No more

**Ruth**  He restoreth my soul –

**Sarah**  Boom boom

**Ruth**  He leadeth me in the paths of righteousness . . .

**Sarah**
Kentucky coffee
Sassafras
Sugar maple
Twisting strange boughs

**Ruth**  I will fear no evil

**Sarah**
Entwined
Knife wind
Cuts through
It is cold

**Ruth**  My cup runs over . . .

# FIFTEEN

*Early morning. The open fields of Saskatchewan.*
*Music.*

**Sarah**
Bitter
Not me
It is old
Old
So old
Not beautiful
Sharp shins wheeling
Turning
Will I
Home
Not home
Not beautiful
No more
Shouldnae be remembered
Boots heavy sludge through
Heavy clay soil
Sun bleeds
Awake
Township of Stanley
Six road ends
Which
Nearly day